Bookmarks Across the Curriculum

Claudette Hegel

Linworth Publishing, Inc.
Worthington, Ohio

This book is dedicated to the staff and students of Poplar Bridge Elementary School in Bloomington, Minnesota. I thank them for the opportunity of volunteering in their media center. Helping students and teachers find information, shelving books, and performing other duties has been interesting, rewarding, and just plain fun.

Library of Congress Cataloging-in-Publication Data

Hegel, Claudette.
   Bookmarks across the curriculum / by Claudette Hegel.
     p. cm.
   Includes index.
   ISBN 1-58683-067-8 (perfectbound)
    1. Elementary school teaching--Handbooks, manuals, etc. 2. Education, Elementary--Miscellanea. 3. Bookmarks. I. Title.

LB1555 .H445 2002
372.19--dc21

                                                                                                                   2002073198

Published by Linworth Publishing, Inc.
480 East Wilson Bridge Road, Suite L
Worthington, Ohio 43085

Copyright © 2002 by Linworth Publishing, Inc.

All rights reserved. Purchasing this book entitles a librarian to reproduce activity sheets for use in the library within a school or entitles a teacher to reproduce activity sheets for single classroom use within a school. Other portions of the book (up to 15 pages) may be copied for staff development purposes within a single school. Standard citation information should appear on each page. The reproduction of any part of this book for an entire school or school system or for commercial use is strictly prohibited. No part of this book may be electronically reproduced, transmitted or recorded without written permission from the publisher.

ISBN: 1-58683-067-8

5 4 3 2 1

Table of Contents

INTRODUCTION iii

SECTION I   Language Arts (60 total bookmarks) 1
                      1. Books and Libraries (11 bookmarks) 1
                      2. Grammar (9 bookmarks) 3
                      3. Parts of Speech (13 bookmarks) 5
                      4. Figures of Speech (14 bookmarks) 8
                      5. Poetry (8 bookmarks) 10
                      6. Writing (5 bookmarks) 12

SECTION II   Math, Time, and Specific Times and Dates (68 total bookmarks) 15
                      7. Math (22 bookmarks) 15
                      8. Time (5 bookmarks) 19
                      9. Specific Times and Dates (41 bookmarks) 20

SECTION III   History and Government (35 total bookmarks) 29
                      10. History (26 bookmarks) 29
                      11. Government (9 bookmarks) 34

SECTION IV   Geography and Famous Places (96 total bookmarks) 37
                      12. The Continents (8 bookmarks) 37
                      13. Countries (14 bookmarks) 39
                      14. States (51 bookmarks) 41
                      15. Miscellaneous Geography (4 bookmarks) 52
                      16. Famous Places and Attractions (19 bookmarks) 52

SECTION V   Physical and Earth Science (43 total bookmarks) 57
                      17. Astronomy (11 bookmarks) 57
                      18. Earth (8 bookmarks) 59
                      19. Weather and Natural Phenomena (14 bookmarks) 61
                      20. Physics (10 bookmarks) 64

SECTION VI   Life Science (112 total bookmarks) 67
                      21. Plants (7 bookmarks) 67
                      22. The Human Body (13 bookmarks) 68
                      23. Ailments and Conditions (8 bookmarks) 71
                      24. Dinosaurs (4 bookmarks) 73
                      25. Mammals (26 bookmarks) 73
                      26. Birds (14 bookmarks) 79
                      27. Amphibians and Reptiles (8 bookmarks) 81
                      28. Crustaceans and Mollusks (8 bookmarks) 83
                      29. Insects (15 bookmarks) 85
                      30. Miscellaneous Animals (9 bookmarks) 88

Table of Contents continued

SECTION VII	Important People (72 total bookmarks)	91
	31. Presidents (42 bookmarks)	91
	32. Explorers (11 bookmarks)	99
	33. Important People (19 bookmarks)	102
SECTION VIII	Daily Life (47 total bookmarks)	107
	34. Languages and Codes (6 bookmarks)	107
	35. Religion (10 bookmarks)	108
	36. Myths and Folklore (18 bookmarks)	110
	37. Clothing and Fashion (5 bookmarks)	114
	38. Foods (8 bookmarks)	115
SECTION IX	Inventions and Technology (40 total bookmarks)	117
	39. Computers (8 bookmarks)	117
	40. Transportation (9 bookmarks)	119
	41. Miscellaneous Inventions (23 bookmarks)	120
SECTION X	Arts and Entertainment (62 total bookmarks)	127
	42. Miscellaneous Arts (9 bookmarks)	127
	43. Music (12 bookmarks)	129
	44. Hobbies and Fun (15 bookmarks)	131
	45. Toys (12 bookmarks)	134
	46. Sports (14 bookmarks)	137
BLANK BOOKMARKS		141
REFERENCES		143
INDEX		147

Introduction

Educators often look for reference materials that provide additional information to help spark their students—interest in learning. Tidbits of trivia and handouts are two ways library media specialists and teachers can reinforce subject material or provide an incentive for research purposes. *Bookmarks Across the Curriculum* combines the two methods to help students learn and to motivate them to want to learn. Each bookmark features educational information or fun facts on a topic related to an upper elementary or middle school curriculum. The bookmarks cover a range of student abilities.

Educators can reproduce the bookmarks in quantities large enough to allow each student to have a copy of every bookmark or in limited quantities to encourage trading as students try to collect each of the bookmarks in a category, such as the 50 states or all the presidents. For collecting purposes, the bookmarks are numbered by sections. The bookmarks can also be used as a "reward" system in which a student who earns a specified number of bookmarks receives a special privilege or bonus.

The bookmarks can be reproduced two-sided to double the information presented to students or reproduced with one side blank. The blank sides on the bookmarks can be used to:

- include additional facts about the subject,
- jot down call numbers, titles, authors, and other information on books found in the card catalog,
- keep track of books read or books to read in the future,
- write notes to students or parents,
- take research notes,
- keep track of school assignments.

Blank bookmarks are included for librarians and teachers to design their own or to emphasize specific material students find difficult. The blank bookmarks may also be given to students who wish to design their own bookmarks. Other students could then photocopy the student-designed bookmarks for use.

If the primary use of the bookmarks is "disposable," such as for notes, school assignments, or card catalog information, they can be reproduced on regular paper. Photocopying bookmarks directly onto heavier paper or even thin cardboard can make them more durable. Or, they can be reproduced on regular paper, then pasted onto heavier paper.

Regardless of how educators use them, the bookmarks in this book provide information on various topics that will help students learn more about subjects across the curriculum and may spark an interest in subjects that students have not previously considered.

SECTION I

Language Arts

BOOKS AND LIBRARIES

The Alphabet

- An alphabet is a set of written symbols, such as letters, that represent sounds that can be combined to form all the words of a language.

- The word *alphabet* is derived from "alpha" and "beta," the first two letters of the Greek alphabet.

- About 3,000 years ago, in 1000 B.C., the Phoenicians invented an alphabet. The English alphabet, as well as most of the other major alphabets in the world, was developed from that alphabet.

- Using the order of an alphabet is a helpful way of organizing items such as books or files.

Bookmark # 1-1

BOOKS AND LIBRARIES

Manuscript Books

- Until printing was developed in the 15th century, each book had to be copied by hand. Many of these manuscript books were copied by monks, who often added elaborate illustrations.

- The monks didn't have erasers and often had to start a page over if they made a mistake.

- Many of the books copied by hand had religious subjects that members of the clergy needed for their church services. Other copied books had useful information, such as plant identification or medical treatments.

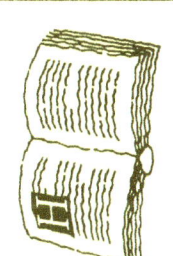

Bookmark # 1-2

BOOKS AND LIBRARIES

Printing

- During the sixth century in China and Japan, people cut words and pictures into wood blocks, dipped or spread ink on the blocks, then pressed the blocks onto paper or cloth.

- In 1438, Johannes Gutenberg used a wine press and jeweler's tools to create a press with moveable type. The first book published in this manner was the Bible. Of the 300 copies of the Gutenberg Bible printed, 47 still exist. Only three of these are considered "perfect."

Bookmark # 1-3

SECTION I: Language Arts | 1

BOOKS AND LIBRARIES

Bibliography

A bibliography can be
- a list of references used in writing a report or other work
- a list of books on a specific subject, such as all known books of bookmarks
- a complete list of a writer's work
- a history of books, authorship, and other book-related subjects, such as a list of all children's books published in the United States before 1900

Bookmark # 1-4

BOOKS AND LIBRARIES

Quotations

A quotation is an interesting phrase, sentence, or even several paragraphs said or written by one person that someone else repeats. Some examples of quotations are

- "Finishing a good book is like leaving a good friend." (William Feather)
- "The first time I read an excellent book, it is to me as if I had gained a new friend." (Oliver Goldsmith)
- "The most exciting words in the English language are 'Once upon a time . . .'" (Katherine Paterson)
- "A book is a sneeze." (E. B. White)

Bookmark # 1-5

BOOKS AND LIBRARIES

Dictionary

- A dictionary is a book containing words of a language, along with their meanings and other information.
- The first dictionaries of modern languages were published in the early 1600s.
- In 1806, Noah Webster became the first person to publish a dictionary in America.
- Words are added to a dictionary and some are dropped on a regular basis. For example, computer terms were added after computers were invented.
- Over 400,000 words appear in an unabridged dictionary.

Bookmark # 1-6

BOOKS AND LIBRARIES

Thesaurus

- A thesaurus is a reference book that lists words that are synonyms (words that mean the same as other words) and sometimes antonyms (words that mean the opposite of other words).
- Some thesauri are in alphabetical order, and others have an index to help locate specific words.
- A thesaurus is a valuable tool for writers and speakers to find just the right words to make their work better.

Bookmark # 1-7

BOOKS AND LIBRARIES

Children's Book Awards

- Caldecott Medal—American Library Association (ALA) award given annually to the illustrator of the "most distinguished picture book"
- Coretta Scott King Award—ALA awards given annually to an African-American author and an African-American illustrator for books considered an "inspirational and educational contribution"
- Newbery Medal—ALA award given annually to the author of the "most distinguished contribution to children's literature"

Bookmark # 1-8

Bookmark # 1-9

BOOKS AND LIBRARIES

Libraries

- In 300 B.C., Ptolemy I of Egypt founded a library of scrolls of papyrus in Alexandria. The library stood for more than 400 years.
- In 1803, the Bingham Library for Youth in Salisbury, Connecticut became the first children's library in America. The library had 150 books for children 9-16 years old.
- The Library of Congress in Washington, DC, has about 20 million books.

Bookmark # 1-10

BOOKS AND LIBRARIES

Library Classification Systems

Most libraries have a way of arranging their books and other items to make them easy to find. The materials are often shelved by subjects. Two of the most popular library systems are

- Dewey decimal system—developed by Melvil Dewey in 1876; uses the numbers 000-999 and their decimals to arrange books in main categories; numbers after decimal points denote subcategories
- Library of Congress system—developed by Herbert Putnam in 1897; uses 21 main classes of letters with numbers for subcategories

Bookmark # 1-11

BOOKS AND LIBRARIES

Dewey Decimal Guide

The Dewey Decimal Classification System organizes books into the following 10 main categories:

- 000-099 General Works (Encyclopedias, Computers, Almanacs, Trivia)
- 100-199 Philosophy, Psychology, Ethics
- 200-299 Religion and Mythology
- 300-399 Sociology
- 400-499 Languages, Dictionaries, Grammar
- 500-599 Science (Math, Chemistry, Biology, Plants, Animals)
- 600-699 Useful Arts (Medicine, Agriculture, Pets, Television)
- 700-799 Fine Arts (Painting, Photography, Music)
- 800-899 Literature, Poetry, Plays
- 900-999 History, Geography, Biography

Bookmark # 2-1

GRAMMAR

Sentences

- Simple sentences have one complete subject (the main noun) and one complete predicate (the verb that creates an action).
- Compound sentences have two or more simple sentences joined with a conjunction (such as "and," "but," or "or") or a semi-colon (;). An example is "I have a lot of math problems to do, and I have to read a lot of history."
- Complex sentences have a simple sentence with at least one dependent clause, such as "After he left the game, his team scored two touchdowns."

sentence + sentence
———————————
compound sentence

Bookmark # 2-2

GRAMMAR

More Sentences

- A declarative sentence makes a statement and ends with a period that looks like this: ".".
- An exclamatory sentence expresses strong emotions and ends with an exclamation point that looks like this: "!".
- An imperative sentence makes a request or command and can end with either a period or an exclamation point.
- An interrogative sentence asks a question and ends with a question mark that looks like this: "?".

SECTION I: Language Arts

GRAMMAR
Punctuation

- apostrophe (')—used in possessive nouns, plurals of letters and words, and contractions to take the place of a missing letter or letters
- colon (:)—used after a greeting in a business letter, between the hours and minutes in a time, to introduce a list or a long direct quotation
- comma (,)—used to separate three or more words or phrases in a series, to set apart appositives, to set off clauses, between the day and year, between the city and state, after the greeting and closing in a letter, with quotations

Bookmark # 2-3

GRAMMAR
More Punctuation

- dash (—)—used to introduce a list of items, before and after any interruption in a sentence
- ellipsis (. . .)—three dots used to show that words have been left out of a sentence; four dots are used if the ellipsis is at the end of a sentence
- exclamation point (!)—used after strong interjections, exclamatory sentences, strong imperative sentences
- hyphen (-)—used in two-part numbers from 21–99 and fractions when written as words, to break a word between syllables at the end of a line, in some compound adjectives and nouns

Bookmark # 2-4

GRAMMAR
Still More Punctuation

- parentheses [( )]—used to add information in a sentence
- period (.)—used after most initials and abbreviations, at the end of some sentences
- question mark (?)—used at the end of an interrogative sentence
- quotation marks—double (" ") used for dialogue, to set apart words or phrases, around some titles; single (' ') used around a quotation written within another quotation
- semicolon (;)—used to join independent clauses, in a series of three or more items when commas are used within the items

Bookmark # 2-5

GRAMMAR
Capitalization

Always capitalize

- the first word in a sentence
- the first, last, and important words of a title
- the pronoun "I"
- a title when before a name (like "Aunt," "Dr.," or "Ms.")
- proper nouns and adjectives
- days of the week
- months of the year
- national and local holidays

Bookmark # 2-6

GRAMMAR
Spelling Rules

- When adding "full" to any word, drop the second *l*. (full of cheer = cheerful)
- When adding *y* or a suffix that begins with a vowel to a word that ends with a silent *e*, drop the silent *e*. (*rose + y* = rosy; *come + ing* = coming)
- When adding a suffix that begins with a consonant, don't drop the silent *e* at the end of a word (*love + ly* = lovely)
- When adding *ing* to a word that ends with *ie*, drop the *e* and change the *i* to *y*. (*tie + ing* = tying)

Bookmark # 2-7

4 | BOOKMARKS ACROSS THE CURRICULUM

PARTS OF SPEECH

ARTICLES

- An article is a word used as an adjective without being descriptive. The three most common articles are "a," "an," and "the."
- A definite article (usually "the") specifies exactly which one. Examples are *the* red car instead of any car and *the* side door instead of any door.
- An indefinite article does not say exactly which one. For example, *a* dog (which could be anything from a poodle to a St. Bernard) or *an* ice cream cone (which could be anything from vanilla to caramel apple peanut delight).

Bookmark # 3-3

PARTS OF SPEECH

ADJECTIVES

Adjectives are words that describe a noun by explaining which one, what kind, or how many. Some examples of adjectives (in italics) are

- *blue suede* shoes
- *heavy* book
- *two small* dogs
- *dozen* eggs
- *playful calico* kitten

What are other adjectives?

Bookmark # 3-2

PARTS OF SPEECH

PARTS OF SPEECH

One way to remember the eight parts of speech is to think of the letters in the name "Ivan Capp."

I — interjection
V — verb
A — adjective
N — noun

C — conjunction
A — adverb
P — preposition
P — pronoun

Bookmark # 3-1

GRAMMAR

What's Wrong?

- The collie runned across the rode.
- We has went too fore football games?
- The Kittens chased there tales
- yesterday my teacher gave us two much homework.
- The hoarse bucked it's rider over the fense.
- I is going to right a letter too my freind.

Bookmark # 2-9

GRAMMAR

More Spelling Rules

- Double the final consonant when adding a suffix that begins with a vowel to a word where the last two letters are a vowel and consonant in that order. (run + ing = running)
- Usually, *i* comes before *e* except after *c*, except when the *ei* sounds like long *a*, such as in "eight" and "vein."
- Some exceptions to all spelling rules occur. Check a dictionary when you do not know the exact spelling.

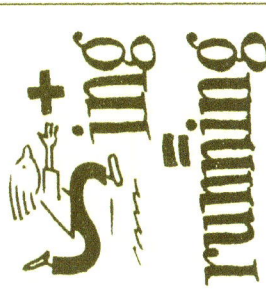

Bookmark # 2-8

SECTION I: Language Arts | 5

PARTS OF SPEECH
ADVERBS

An adverb is a word or phrase that describes a verb. Some examples of adverbs are

- sweetly (tells how)
- faster than a speeding bullet (tells how)
- tomorrow (tells when)
- five years ago (tells when)
- up (tells where)
- through the keyhole (tells where)
- twice (tells how often)
- once in a blue moon (tells how often)

What are other adverbs?

_____
_____
_____

Bookmark # 3-4

PARTS OF SPEECH
CONJUNCTIONS

- A conjunction is a word that joins sentences or combines ideas. The ideas can be phrases, clauses, or single words.
- A coordinating conjunction is used when the idea on each side of the conjunction is of equal importance. Examples of coordinating conjunctions include "and," "but," and "or."
- Subordinating conjunctions join two parts of a sentence that aren't of equal importance. Some subordinating conjunctions are "after," "although," "as," "because," "before," "if," "since," "so," "unless," "until," "when," and "while."

Bookmark # 3-5

PARTS OF SPEECH
INTERJECTIONS

- An interjection is a word that shows strong feelings, from excitement to pain to joy to sorrow.
- An interjection is often more like a sound than a word.
- Interjections are often followed by an exclamation point.
- Some examples of interjections are "awesome," "golly," "hooray," "ouch," "tsk-tsk," "uh-oh," "whew," "wow," and "yuck."

Bookmark # 3-6

PARTS OF SPEECH
NOUNS

A noun is a word that means a person, place, or thing. Every complete sentence needs at least one noun. In a sentence, a noun can be

- the subject, in which the noun is the main person, place, or thing
- the direct object of a prepositional phrase, or the direct object of the entire sentence, in which the noun follows a verb and completes the meaning of the sentence
- the indirect object, in which the noun tells to whom or what, or for whom or what something was done

Bookmark # 3-7

PARTS OF SPEECH
PROPER NOUNS

Proper nouns name specific persons, animals, places, or things. Proper nouns always begin with a capital letter. Some examples are

- Maurice Sendak (person)
- Dr. Seuss (person)
- Sounder (dog)
- Poplar Bridge Elementary School (place—specific building)
- Powderhorn Park (place—recreation area)
- McClusky, North Dakota (place—town and state)
- American Library Association (thing—organization)
- *Charlotte's Web* (thing—book)
- Declaration of Independence (thing—political document)

Bookmark # 3-8

---

6 | BOOKMARKS ACROSS THE CURRICULUM

PARTS OF SPEECH
IRREGULAR VERBS

Irregular verbs can't be made into past tense simply by adding *ed* at the end of the verb. Instead, the word itself changes, sometimes only slightly, but other times completely. Some examples of irregular verbs are

- do, did, done
- drive, drove, driven
- go, went, gone
- hide, hid, hidden
- ride, rode, ridden
- ring, rang, rung
- see, saw, seen
- sing, sang, sung
- write, wrote, written

Bookmark # 3-13

PARTS OF SPEECH
VERB TENSES

- Present tense tells what is happening now. The verb often ends in *s*. An example is "The dog barks loudly."
- Past tense tells what has already happened. The verb often ends in *ed*. An example is "The dog barked loudly yesterday."
- Future tense tells what is going to happen. The word *will* usually comes before the verb. An example is "The dog will bark loudly tomorrow."

Bookmark # 3-12

PARTS OF SPEECH
VERBS

- Every sentence needs a verb, which is a word that shows action. A verb explains what something does, such as "sings," or that something exists, such as "is."
- Intransitive verbs can stand alone because the meaning is complete. An example is "purred" in the sentence "The cat purred."
- Transitive verbs need an object to complete the meaning. An example is the verb in the sentence "The cat chased the mouse." (The "chased" needs "the mouse" to complete the sentence.)

Bookmark # 3-11

PARTS OF SPEECH
PRONOUNS

- A pronoun is a word that takes the place of a noun.
- Like a noun, a pronoun can be the subject, direct object, indirect object, or object of a preposition. Most pronouns refer to people or animals, but a few refer to inanimate objects.
- Some examples of pronouns are "he," "her," "him," "I," "it," "me," "mine," "she," "them," "they," "us," "we," and "you."

Bookmark # 3-10

PARTS OF SPEECH
PREPOSITIONS

A preposition comes before a noun or pronoun, along with any adjectives, to show the relationship of that noun or pronoun to some other word in the sentence. An example is "up" in the sentence "The squirrel ran up the tree." Some other prepositions are "across," "at," "below," "between," "by," "for," "in," "of," "off," "on," "out," "over," and "to."

Bookmark # 3-9

SECTION I: Language Arts 7

FIGURES OF SPEECH

ANTONYMS

An antonym is a word that means the opposite of another word. Some examples of antonyms are

- big, little
- difficult, easy
- fast, slow
- hard, soft
- loud, quiet
- open, closed
- right, wrong

What are other antonyms?

_____
_____
_____

Bookmark # 4-1

HOMONYMS

Homonyms are words that have the same sound, but have different meanings and are usually spelled differently. Some examples of homonyms are

- ate, eight
- blew, blue
- dear, deer
- new, knew
- sew, so
- to, too, two

What are other homonyms?

_____
_____
_____

Bookmark # 4-2

SYNONYMS

A synonym is a word that has the same or a similar meaning as another word. Some examples of synonyms are

- box, carton, case, package
- cry, bawl, sob, wail, weep, whimper
- funny, amusing, humorous, laughable
- little, itty-bitty, short, small, teeny, tiny, wee
- stop, cease, end, halt, quit, terminate

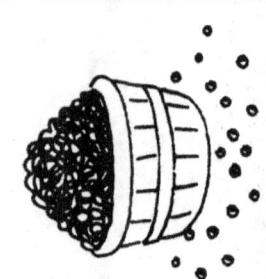

Bookmark # 4-3

ALLITERATION

Alliteration is a figure of speech with repeated sounds at the beginning of two or more words or syllables. Some examples of alliteration are

- big blueberry basket
- cat claws cause cuts
- Diana's delicious dessert
- pansy's pretty petals
- wind's wild wonder

What are other examples of alliteration?

Bookmark # 4-4

ASSONANCE

Assonance is a figure of speech in which a vowel sound is repeated in two or more words. Some examples of assonance are

- cat can dance
- same rare plane
- Ben met Mel
- bees see me
- Jim is kidding Rick
- white pipe shines
- top dog jogs
- Joe's note
- sun's up
- Hugh chews through stew

Bookmark # 4-5

---

8 | BOOKMARKS ACROSS THE CURRICULUM

FIGURES OF SPEECH
CLICHÉS

A cliché is an expression that has been overused. Some examples of clichés are

- as the crow flies
- dead as a doornail
- hit the nail on the head
- lower than a snake's belly
- old as the hills
- packed in like sardines
- raining cats and dogs
- sly as a fox

Bookmark # 4-6

FIGURES OF SPEECH
CONSONANCE

Consonance is a figure of speech that repeats consonant sounds in two or more words or syllables. The words don't have to rhyme, but sometimes do. Some examples of consonance are

- bananas
- different photographs
- maybe enemy's memories minimal
- Mississippi
- remember arrows are really sharp

What are other examples of consonance?

Bookmark # 4-7

FIGURES OF SPEECH
HYPERBOLE

Hyperbole is a figure of speech that describes something through exaggeration. Some examples of hyperbole are

- I'm so hungry I could eat a horse.
- These books weigh a ton.
- I'm so happy I could burst.
- He's so angry, steam is coming out of his ears.
- I've told you a million times not to exaggerate so much.

Bookmark # 4-8

FIGURES OF SPEECH
IDIOMS

An idiom is a phrase that means something different from its literal meaning. Some examples of idioms are

- ants in your pants (not bugs in your britches, but you can't sit still)
- ear to the ground (not getting your ear dirty, but listening)
- go out on a limb (not be in a tree, but take a chance)
- head in the clouds (not really tall, but thinking isn't "down-to-earth")
- keep your nose to the grindstone (not filing your nose, but keep working steadily)

Bookmark # 4-9

FIGURES OF SPEECH
METAPHORS

A metaphor is a figure of speech in which a word, always a noun, is used in place of another to suggest a likeness between them. Some examples of metaphors are

- classroom is a zoo
- comedian is a riot
- lake is a mirror
- nurse is an angel
- snow is a white blanket

What are other metaphors?

Bookmark # 4-10

SECTION I: Language Arts | 9

POETRY

Poetry

Poetry is writing using rhythms, patterns of sound, and often imagery. Poetry, either rhymed or unrhymed, can be more than pleasing language.

Poetry

- can express a feeling or show imagination with descriptive words
- can make a complicated idea easier to understand
- sometimes tells a story
- often offers praises to nature, God, a person, or something else
- can be silly or funny
- can be a way to teach

Bookmark # 5-1

FIGURES OF SPEECH

Tongue Twisters

A tongue twister is a sentence or phrase that is difficult to pronounce when quickly repeated several times because of the similarity in sounds. Some examples of tongue twisters are

- How much wood would a woodchuck chuck if a woodchuck could chuck wood?
- Rubber baby buggy bumpers
- She sells seashells by the seashore.

Bookmark # 4-14

FIGURES OF SPEECH

Similes

A simile is a figure of speech in which two things are compared by the use of the word *like* or *as*. Some examples of similes are

- cried like a baby
- ran like the wind
- teeth chattered like castanets
- fog as thick as pea soup
- hair soft as silk
- smile as bright as the sun

What are other examples of similes?

_____
_____
_____

Bookmark # 4-13

FIGURES OF SPEECH

Personification

Personification is a figure of speech that gives human characteristics to nonhuman things. Some examples of personification are

- The moon looks over the valley.
- The tiger smiled when leaving his cage.
- The rock guarded the entrance to the cave.
- The running water skipped over the rocks.
- Autumn leaves danced in the breeze.

Bookmark # 4-12

FIGURES OF SPEECH

Onomatopoeia

Onomatopoeia is a word that sounds like the noise the word represents. Some examples of onomatopoeia are

- bark (like a dog)
- clang
- crash
- cuckoo
- meow
- moo
- purr
- splash

What are other examples of onomatopoeia?

_____
_____
_____

Bookmark # 4-11

---

10 | BOOKMARKS ACROSS THE CURRICULUM

POETRY

LIMERICK

A limerick is a five-line poem, usually funny, in which the first, second, and fifth lines rhyme, and the third and fourth lines complete another rhyme. An example is

*There once was a man from Bismarck
Who fell asleep in the park
He started to snore
As loud as a roar
And scared everyone until dark.*

Bookmark # 5-6

HAIKU

A haiku, which originated in Japan, is a three-line poem that is usually about nature. A haiku often has five syllables in the first and third lines, and seven syllables in the second line, for a total of seventeen syllables. An example is

*gold and russet leaves
swirling twirling and tumbling
playing in the wind*

Write another haiku.

_____
_____
_____
_____
_____

Bookmark # 5-5

FREE VERSE

Free verse is unrhymed poetry with no special rules for structure, length, punctuation, or anything else. The author can be completely "free" while writing the poem. An example is

*snow melting fast on
a warm spring day
the bottom boughs
of a pine tree
break free from
the snowbank
and jump
for joy*

Bookmark # 5-4

DIAMANTÉ POEM

A diamanté poem is written with either five or seven lines in a diamond shape. The first line is one subject and the last line is another subject. Each word is somehow related to the ones just before and just after it. Usually the two subjects are also related. An example is

*cat
warm soft
furry cuddly friendly
loyal obedient
dog*

Bookmark # 5-3

CINQUAIN POEM

A cinquain poem has five lines with a set number of syllables and a specific rule for each line.

- The first line has two syllables (often only one word) and names the subject.
- The second line has four syllables and describes the subject.
- The third line has six syllables and describes the subject's action.
- The fourth line has eight syllables and describes a feeling about the subject.
- The fifth line has two syllables (often only one word) and gives another name for the subject.

Bookmark # 5-2

SECTION I: Language Arts | 11

POETRY

Pattern Poetry

In pattern poetry, the word or line arrangement creates a design or shape, usually something suggested by the words. In the following example, the slanting lines echo the idea of slanting rain.

slanting rain
hits the window
like nature's fingers
rapping on the glass

Bookmark # 5-7

POETRY

Quinzaine Poem

A quinzaine is a poem with 15 syllables in three lines that don't rhyme. The first line makes a statement, and the next two lines ask a question about the subject. An example is

The quarterback threw a pass.
Should he have called a running play?

Write another quinzaine.

_____
_____
_____
_____
_____

Bookmark # 5-8

WRITING

Book Report

How to write a book report:

- Choose a book, read it carefully, and think about what you read.
- Organize your ideas in your mind or on paper.
- Tell a little about the book.
- Explain why you did or didn't like the book.
- Include the title and author of the book in your report.

Bookmark # 6-1

WRITING

Diaries, Journals, Reminiscences

- A diary is a description of activities or thoughts written on a regular basis, usually daily.
- A journal is similar to a diary, although journal entries are usually longer and more detailed than in a diary.
- Reminiscences are simply memories. Often people will detail their reminiscences in written essays or stories.

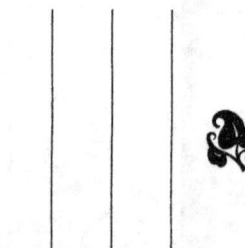

Bookmark #6-2

WRITING

Reports

Steps in writing a report:

1. Choose a subject. It's best to choose a subject you find interesting.
2. Look for information in books, magazines, newspapers, on the Internet, and other sources.
3. Take notes—don't forget to keep track of the sources for your bibliography.
4. Prepare an outline, which is an organized plan of the report.
5. Write the report.
6. Prepare a bibliography (a list of your references).
7. Check for errors in organization, meaning, spelling, punctuation, and grammar. Then rewrite the report.

Bookmark # 6-3

---

12 | BOOKMARKS ACROSS THE CURRICULUM

WRITING

Hints for Writers

- Keep a journal of your experiences, thoughts, and feelings, no matter how ordinary they seem at the time.
- Try to keep a regular writing schedule.
- Include each of the five senses in your stories.
- Think about the five *W*s (who, what, where, when, and why [or how]).
- Write to please yourself first.
- Ideas can be found from personal experiences, dreams (either during sleep or daydreams), pictures or photographs, and asking "What if . . . ?"

Bookmark # 6-5

WRITING

Speeches

- A speech is "the communication of thoughts in spoken words," meant to be heard instead of read. Speeches do not have to be written down, but they usually are written first.
- Good speeches can be informative, funny, convincing, or inspiring.
- Good speeches make specific points.
- Speeches should be composed for the audience instead of for the speaker.
- An audience will provide positive feedback to a good speech.

Bookmark # 6-4

SECTION I: Language Arts | 13

Section II

Math, Time, and Specific Times and Dates

Bookmark # 7-3

MATH
How Much is a Million?

Try this math experiment:

1. Use an eyedropper to count the number of drops in a tablespoon.
2. To find the number of drops in a cup, count the number of tablespoons in a cup and multiply by the number of drops in a tablespoon.
3. Determine the number of drops in a pint, then quart, and finally gallon.
4. How many gallons are needed for one million drops?

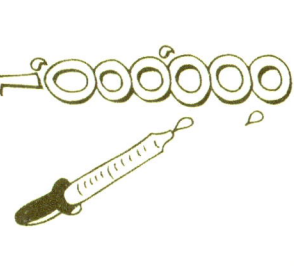

Bookmark # 7-2

MATH
Number Magic

Try this math experiment:

1. Pick a number from 1 to 9.
2. Multiply the number by 5.
3. Add 3 to the total.
4. Multiply that total by 2.
5. Pick another number from 1 to 9.
6. Add that number to the previous total.
7. Subtract 6.

The answer should be the two numbers you picked in order. Try the experiment again using two other numbers.

Bookmark # 7-1

MATH
Numbers

- Numbers have an order and are infinite, which means they go on forever because one more always can be added to the highest number known.
- Numbers can be used to indicate quantity, such as "25 students," or order, such as "the third day."
- Before numbers were invented, people used their fingers, twigs, or stones to scratch lines in the dirt to indicate quantity. The word *calculate* comes from a Latin word for stone.
- The most popular number systems are based on 10 because that's the number of fingers people have.

1, 2, 3

Roman Numerals

Letters of the Roman alphabet were used as symbols for numbers until the 15th century. The letters representing numbers are

I = 1
V = 5
X = 10
L = 50
C = 100
D = 500
M = 1,000

One letter can be placed in front of another of greater value to be subtracted from it. One or more letters can be placed after a letter to be added to it. Examples are IV = 4 (5 - 1), VI = 6 (5 + 1), and XCVIII = 98 (100 - 10 + 5 + 3).

Bookmark # 7-4

Adding and Subtracting

- Addition is combining two or more numbers. Adding is represented by a plus sign (+). An example of an addition equation is "2 + 3 = 5" (two plus three equals five).

- Subtraction is taking a number away from another number. Subtracting is represented by a minus sign (-). An example of a subtraction equation is "9 - 6 = 3" (nine minus six equals three).

- Addition and subtraction equations can also be listed vertically (with the numbers listed up-and-down) instead of across.

Bookmark # 7-5

Multiplying and Dividing

- Multiplication is adding equal numbers repeatedly in only one step. Multiplying is represented by a multiplication sign (x). For example, "3 + 3 + 3 + 3 + 3" can be simply "3 x 5" (three times five).

- Division is used to discover how many times one number goes into another number. Dividing is represented by a division sign (÷). The divisor is the number that goes into the dividend. In "12 ÷ 4" (twelve divided by four), the 4 is the divisor and the 12 is the dividend.

Bookmark # 7-6

Multiplication Fun

Use a calculator to multiply 142,857 by the following numbers and see what happens:

1 = _____
2 = _____
3 = _____
4 = _____
5 = _____
6 = _____

Now multiply 12,345,679 (notice the 8 is missing) by

27 = _____
36 = _____
45 = _____
54 = _____
55 = _____
66 = _____
69 = _____
and
1,371,742 x 9= _____
9.739369 x 9= _____

Bookmark # 7-7

Division Fun

Divide the following numbers by 11 and see what happens:

34 = _____
56 = _____
78 = _____
89 = _____
122 = _____
10 = _____
20 = _____
30 = _____
40 = _____
50 = _____
60 = _____
70 = _____
80 = _____
90 = _____
100 = _____

Bookmark # 7-8

MATH

Adding and Subtracting Decimals

To add or subtract decimals, simply line up the decimal points in the numbers whether the decimals have tenths, hundredths, or thousandths. Consider any blank place as 0.

Examples:

```
  20.43
 140.8
  +3.692
 ──────
 164.922
```

★ ★

```
 136.45
 -21.978
 ──────
 114.472
```

Find the answer to

```
  24.7
   8.316
+152.96
```

Bookmark # 7-13

MATH

Decimals

- Decimals show a part of a whole and are written with a decimal point that looks like the period at the end of this sentence. The whole number is to the left of the decimal point, and the part of a whole is to the right of the decimal point.

- One position to the right of the decimal point is tenths of a whole, two positions to the right is hundredths, and three positions to the right is thousandths.

- A hint: think of decimals in the hundredths as pennies in a dollar. For example, the number 1.57 would be one dollar and fifty-seven cents if it were money.

Bookmark # 7-12

MATH

A Math Mystery

- A pet store had 17 puppies. A woman asked for one-half of the puppies. A man asked for one-third of the puppies. A boy asked for one-ninth of the puppies.

- The store owner didn't know how to divide the puppies evenly, so he added a kitten to the mix to make a total of 18 pets.

- The woman got one-half of the 18 pets, or 9 puppies.

- The man got one-third of the 18 pets, or 6 puppies.

- The boy got one-ninth of the 18 pets, or 2 puppies.

- That totaled 17 pets, so the owner put the kitten back in its cage.

Bookmark # 7-11

MATH

Fractions

- A fraction is a number that represents part of a whole, such as ½ (one-half) or ¼ (one-fourth or one-quarter). The top number is called a numerator. The bottom number is called a denominator.

- To add or subtract fractions, the denominator must be the same.

- To multiply a fraction, first multiply the numerators, then multiply the denominators.

- To divide a fraction, reverse the positions of the numerator and denominator of the divisor (the second fraction), then multiply the two fractions.

$\frac{3}{4}$

Bookmark # 7-10

MATH

Math Facts

- Add any two odd numbers. The answer will always be even.

- Subtract any even number from any odd number. The answer will always be odd.

- Subtract any odd number from any other odd number. The answer will always be even.

- Multiply any even number by any other number, odd or even. The answer will always be even.

- Multiply any odd number by any other odd number. The answer will always be odd.

- Multiply any number ending in 5 by any other number also ending in 5. The answer will always end in 5.

Bookmark # 7-9

SECTION II: Math, Times, and Specific Times and Dates | 17

MATH: Multiplying and Dividing Decimals

- When multiplying decimals, multiply the numbers as if the decimals weren't there. Count the number of places to the right of the decimal points in the numbers multiplied. Put the decimal point that many places from the far right of the answer.
- When dividing decimals, move the decimal point of the divisor (the number outside the bracket) to the right to make it a whole number. Then move the decimal of the dividend (the number inside the bracket) the same number of positions, adding as many zeros as necessary.

.00000

Bookmark # 7-14

MATH: Averages

To find an average, add each of the numbers in a group and divide by the number of items in that group. For example, the average of 22, 56, and 87 is 55 (22 + 56 + 87 = 165; 165 ÷ 3 = 55).

- Find the average high temperature over a week if the daily high temperatures were 78, 81, 79, 77, 80, 76, and 75. Answer
- Find the average grade for homework assignments graded 96, 84, 87, 94, 100, 92, 88, 93, and 85. Answer
- Other averages to find: number of pages in several books, number of students per class in your school, and age of students in your class.

Bookmark # 7-15

MATH: Graphs

- A bar graph may have either horizontal or vertical bars to show the data (information) comparisons.
- A line graph has dots or points with a connecting line to show the data comparisons.
- A pictograph uses rows of symbols or pictures (such as books to show how many books are in a library) to show data comparisons. Pictographs are often unable to represent exact numbers.
- A pie graph uses a circular shape and divides the information into sections like different-sized pieces of a pie.

PIE GRAPH

Bookmark # 7-16

MATH: Graphing Fun

Determine which type of graph would be best for the following subjects and select a graph to make:

- color of shirts students in the class are wearing
- birthdays of class members
- types of pets (or stuffed animals) class members have
- differences in number of boys, girls, and teachers in your school
- class members' favorite school subjects
- number of books on several shelves in the media center

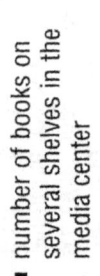

Bookmark # 7-17

MATH: Geometry

- A square has four equal sides.
- A rectangle has four equal angles (corners) and four sides; the parallel sides must be equal in length, although all four sides do not have to be equal.
- A triangle has three sides and angles.
- A circle is round with all edges the same distance from the center.
- A hexagon has six sides and six angles.

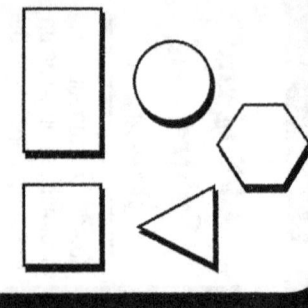
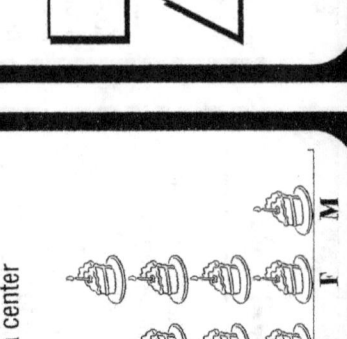

Bookmark # 7-18

18 BOOKMARKS ACROSS THE CURRICULUM

T I M E

Intervals of Time

- 60 seconds = 1 minute
- 60 minutes = 1 hour
- 24 hours = 1 day
- 7 days = 1 week
- 4 to 4½ weeks (about 30 days) = 1 month
- 12 months (about 365 days or 52 weeks) = 1 year
- 10 years = 1 decade
- 20 years = 1 score
- 100 years = 1 century
- 1,000 years = 1 millennium

Bookmark # 8-1

MATH

Metric Measurements

Length:
- meter = about 39.37 inches
- centimeter = 1/100 of a meter or 0.4 inches
- millimeter = 1/1000 of a meter or 0.04 inches
- kilometer = 1,000 meters or about 0.6 mile, 3,168 feet, or 1,056 yards

Weight:
- gram = 0.035 ounce
- centigram = 1/100 of a gram or 0.00035 ounce
- milligram = 1/1000 of a gram or 0.000035 ounce
- kilogram = 1,000 grams or about 2.2 pounds

Bookmark # 7-22

MATH

Measurement— Light Year

The universe is so large that measuring distances in miles is difficult. Instead of measuring in miles, the distances in the universe are measured by light years. A light year is the distance a beam of light travels in one year—that's 5,880,000,000,000 miles. The Milky Way's diameter is 100,000 light years or 588,000,000,000,000,000 miles.

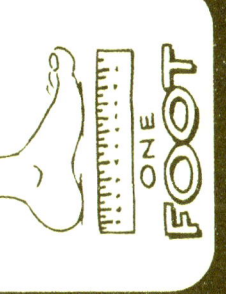

Bookmark # 7-21

MATH

Measurements

- A foot is 12 inches long because the measurement is based on the length of the foot of the man who started using that measurement.
- In the 12th century, Henry I of England established a yard as a distance from the tip of a man's nose to the tip of his outstretched thumb. Edward I standardized the length to 3 feet (36 inches) in 1305.
- The Romans set the distance for a mile at 1,000 paces or 5,000 feet, which was later standardized to 5,280 feet (1,760 yards).

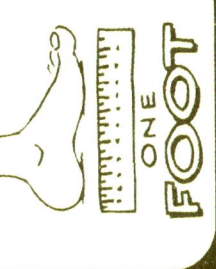

Bookmark # 7-20

MATH

Geometry Formulas

- area of a square = length x width
- diameter of a circle = radius x 2
- circumference of a circle = pi (a mathematical symbol for 3.14) x diameter
- area of a circle = pi x radius^2 (or radius x radius)

What's the area of a square 5 feet long and 4 feet wide? _____ square feet

What's the circumference of a circle with a radius of 2 inches? _____ inches

What's the area of a circle with a diameter of 6 inches? _____ square inches

Bookmark # 7-19

SECTION II: Math, Times, and Specific Times and Dates

SPECIFIC TIMES & DATES

Days of the Week

- Sunday means "day of the sun."
- Monday comes from the Anglo-Saxon word *Monadaeg*, which means "the day of the moon."
- Tuesday is named for Tyr, the Norse god of war.
- Wednesday is named for the Norse god of storms, Wodin, Woden, or Odin.
- Thursday is named for Thor, the Norse god of thunder.
- Friday is named for Freya, the wife of the Norse god Odin.
- Saturday is named for Saturn, the Roman god who ruled over planting.

Bookmark # 9-1

TIME — Calendars

- Each year Americans use more than 120 million wall calendars and 300 million desk calendars. Those numbers do not include wallet, hand-made, or perpetual (can be used in any year) calendars.
- Calendars come in a variety of styles and sizes. Some calendars feature an entire year or more in one section, while others are divided into months, weeks, days, and even hours.
- One type of calendar is a 12-sided block with one side for each month. Sometimes the block calendar has a slot in it to use as a bank.

Bookmark # 8-5

TIME — Watches

- A Swiss watchmaker made the first wristwatch in 1790. He noticed that a woman in the park had a pocket watch tied around her wrist so that she could use both hands to care for her child.
- Most watches used to be carried in a pants or vest pocket until 1900 when wristwatches became more popular.
- In 1914, a wristwatch shown at an exhibit in Switzerland was called "just a passing fancy." Now wristwatches are the most popular jewelry item in the world.

Bookmark # 8-4

TIME — Clocks

- The first clock was built around 1360. That clock ran about two hours fast or slow each day.
- Early clocks had only one hand: the hour hand.
- Clocks can be powered by electricity, batteries (including solar-powered batteries), or a pendulum or a similar device that uses gravity to create a continual force.
- Many clocks are now digital instead of having a clock face.
- Benjamin Franklin suggested setting clocks ahead for daylight saving time as a joke, but others took him seriously.

Bookmark # 8-3

TIME — Sundials

Sundials are used to tell time using the position and angle of the sun to create a shadow on a specially-designed device. The sundial is often roughly circular with a central indicator (called a gnomon) and numbers around the outside similar to a clock. Wherever the gnomon's shadow falls is the time. The sundial must be set up in a certain position so that the reading is correct.

Bookmark # 8-2

BOOKMARKS ACROSS THE CURRICULUM

January

- January is named for the Roman god Janus, who protects gates and doorways. Janus is often pictured with two faces, one looking into the past and the other into the future.
- Some special days in January include
  - New Year's Day (1st)
  - Twelfth Night (5th)
  - Martin Luther King Day (15th; celebrated on the third Monday)
  - Super Bowl Sunday (date varies)
  - (Presidential) Inauguration Day (20th) (every fourth year)

Bookmark # 9-2

February

- February is named for the Roman month Februalia, a month of purification and atonement. The Latin word *februare* means "to cleanse."
- February is African-American History Month.
- Some special days in February include
  - Groundhog Day (2nd)
  - Valentine's Day (14th)
  - Lincoln's Birthday (12th)
  - Washington's Birthday (February 22nd)
  - Presidents' Day (third Monday)
  - Mardi Gras (date varies)

Bookmark # 9-3

March

- The month of March is named for Mars, the Roman god of war. During Ancient Roman times, March was the time of year to resume the military campaigns that winter interrupted.
- March is National Women's History Month.
- Some special days in March include
  - St. Patrick's Day (17th)
  - official beginning of spring (around the 20th)
  - Palm Sunday, Maundy Thursday, Good Friday, Easter, and Passover, each of which sometimes occur in March and sometimes in April

Bookmark # 9-4

April

- April is named for the Latin word *aperire*, which means "to open (or bud)." Many plants begin to grow in April.
- April is Keep America Beautiful Month, Mathematics Education Month, Prevention of Cruelty to Animals Month, and School Library Media Month.
- National Library Week is generally the second full week of April.
- The last full week of April is National TV-Free (turn off the TV) Week and National Volunteer Week.
- Some special days in April include
  - April Fool's Day (1st)
  - International Children's Book Day (2nd)
  - Set-Your-Clock-Forward Day (beginning of Daylight Savings Time—first Sunday)

Bookmark # 9-5

May

- May is named for the Roman goddess Maia, who oversaw the growth of plants.
- The first full week of May is Be Kind to Animals Week and PTA Teacher Appreciation Week.
- National Police Week is the week including May 15.
- Some special days in May include
  - May Day (1st)
  - Cinco de Mayo (5th)
  - V-E Day (8th)
  - National Teacher Day (first or second Tuesday)
  - Mother's Day (second Sunday)
  - Memorial Day (the last Monday)

Bookmark # 9-6

SECTION II: *Math, Times, and Specific Times and Dates* | 21

Bookmark # 9-7

Monday 22 — SPECIFIC TIMES & DATES

June

- June is named for the Roman goddess Juno, the guardian of marriage and the well being of women. June is a popular month for weddings.
- Some special days in June include
  - D Day (6th)
  - World Environment Day (5th)
  - Flag Day (14th)
  - Father's Day (third Sunday)
  - official beginning of summer (around the 20th)

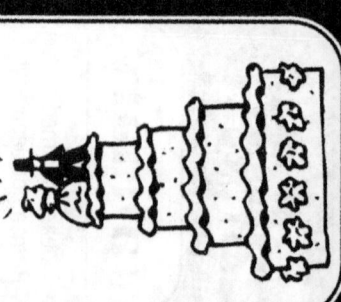

Bookmark # 9-8

Monday 22 — SPECIFIC TIMES & DATES

July

- July is named for the Roman dictator Julius Caesar, who developed the Julian calendar.
- July is both National Hot Dog Month and National Ice Cream Month.
- Some special days in July include
  - Independence Day (4th)
  - Bastille Day (14th)
  - Moon Day, the anniversary of Neil Armstrong and Edwin "Buzz" Aldrin, Jr.'s, walk on the moon (20th)

Bookmark # 9-9

Monday 22 — SPECIFIC TIMES & DATES

August

- The month of August is named for Augustus Caesar, the first Roman emperor.
- The first week of August is International Clown Week.
- Some special days in August include
  - Coast Guard Day (4th)
  - International Left-hander's Day (13th)
  - National Aviation Day (19th)

Bookmark # 9-10

Monday 22 — SPECIFIC TIMES & DATES

September

- September is named for the Latin word *septem*, which means "seven." This was the seventh month of the early Roman calendar.
- September is Library Card Sign-up Month and National Literacy Month.
- The last week of September is Banned Books Week—Celebrating the Freedom to Read.
- Some special days in September include
  - Labor Day (first Monday)
  - Mayflower Day (16th)
  - Constitution/Citizenship Day (17th)
  - official beginning of autumn (around the 20th)

Bookmark # 9-11

Monday 22 — SPECIFIC TIMES & DATES

October

- October is named from the Latin word *octo*, which means "eight." This was the eighth month of the early Roman calendar.
- October is Fire Prevention Month, National Youth Against Tobacco Month, and Vegetarian Awareness Month.
- Some special days in October include
  - Columbus Day (traditionally the 12th; celebrated on the Monday near the day)
  - United Nations Day (24th)
  - Navy Day (27th)
  - Change-Your-Clock-Back Day (end of Daylight Savings Time—last Sunday)
  - Halloween (31st)

SPECIFIC TIMES & DATES
Monday 22

November

- The month of November is named for the Latin word *novem*, which means "nine." This was the ninth month of the early Roman calendar.
- November is Peanut Butter Lover's Month.
- The third week of November is National Children's Book Week.
- Some special days in November include
  - Election Day (first Tuesday after the first Monday)
  - Veteran's Day (11th)
  - Great American Smokeout (third Thursday)
  - Thanksgiving (fourth Thursday)

Bookmark # 9-12

SPECIFIC TIMES & DATES
Monday 22

December

- December is named for the Latin word *decem*, which means "ten." This was the tenth month of the early Roman calendar.
- Some special days in December include
  - Pearl Harbor Remembrance Day (7th)
  - official beginning of winter (around the 22nd)
  - Christmas Eve (24th)
  - Christmas Day (25th)
  - Kwanzaa (26th; lasts for 7 days)
  - Boxing Day (26th)
  - New Year's Eve (31st)
  - Hanukkah (date varies)

Bookmark # 9-13

SPECIFIC TIMES & DATES
Monday 22

New Year's Day

- Many people in countries around the world don't celebrate New Year's Day on January 1 as those in the United States do. The Chinese New Year begins in January or February. The Buddhist New Year begins in March or April. The Jewish New Year begins in September or October.
- A former New Year's Day custom was to go caroling, and offer gifts of apples or oranges either rolled in oatmeal or stuck with nutmeg or cloves, then topped with mistletoe. The "Apple Gift" was used for decoration.

Bookmark # 9-14

SPECIFIC TIMES & DATES
Monday 22

Martin Luthur King, Jr.'s Birthday

- Martin Luther King, Jr. was born on January 15, 1929. In 1986, Congress set aside the third Monday in January to honor King.
- Dr. King, a minister, gave his famous "I Have a Dream" speech in Washington, DC, in 1963. His closing words "Free at last/ Free at last/Thank God Almighty/I'm free at last" are from an old slave song.
- In 1964, at age 35, King became the youngest person to receive the Nobel Peace Prize.
- King was assassinated in Memphis, Tennessee, on April 4, 1968.

Bookmark # 9-15

SPECIFIC TIMES & DATES
Monday 22

Inauguration Day

- An official ceremony takes place the day a U.S. president takes an oath of office.
- George Washington was inaugurated as the first president of the United States on April 30, 1789.
- Starting with the second president, John Adams, the term of the President began on March 4.
- In 1933, the adoption of the 20th Amendment to the Constitution changed the day the president takes office to January 20. Harry S. Truman was the first president who began his term on January 20.

Bookmark # 9-16

SECTION II: Math, Times, and Specific Times and Dates | 23

SPECIFIC TIMES & DATES
Monday 22

Chinese New Year

- The Chinese New Year begins at sunset after the day of the second new moon following the winter solstice. This day occurs between January 21 and February 19 each year. The celebration lasts from a week to a month.
- Each Chinese year is represented by one of the animals of the Chinese Zodiac. The animals include monkey, cock, dog, pig, rat, ox, tiger, hare, dragon, serpent, horse, and sheep.
- Celebrations for the Chinese New Year usually include fireworks.

Bookmark # 9-17

SPECIFIC TIMES & DATES
Monday 22

Groundhog Day

- Groundhog Day is observed on February 2. According to tradition, if a groundhog, also known as a woodchuck or a whistle pig, comes out of its burrow and sees its shadow on this day, winter will last another six weeks. If the day is cloudy and the groundhog doesn't see its shadow, spring will soon arrive.
- Immigrants from Great Britain and Germany brought the custom of Groundhog Day to the United States, although the badger instead of the groundhog was the traditional animal used.

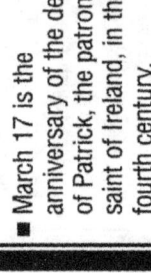

Bookmark # 9-18

SPECIFIC TIMES & DATES
Monday 22

St. Valentine's Day

- February 14 is the traditional day of romance. The holiday is named for a Catholic priest who made many sacrifices for love.
- People once believed that February 14 was the day birds chose their mates.
- During an Ancient Roman festival, names of young men and women were put into a box on Valentine's Day. A random drawing paired a man and a woman for the year.

Bookmark # 9-19

SPECIFIC TIMES & DATES
Monday 22

President's Day

- At one time, separate holidays for Abraham Lincoln's birthday on February 12 and George Washington's birthday on February 22 were observed.
- Although some states still observe both Lincoln's and Washington's birthdays, the national holiday combines the days into Presidents' Day, which is celebrated on the third Monday in February.
- Many people honor all presidents on Presidents' Day, not just Washington and Lincoln.
- One way people honor Washington is by eating cherry pie in recognition of the legend that he chopped down a cherry tree in his youth.

Bookmark # 9-20

SPECIFIC TIMES & DATES
Monday 22

St. Patrick's Day

- St. Patrick's Day, on March 17, is the traditional date for the Irish and Irish-Americans to celebrate by wearing green, and organizing parades, parties, and dances.
- March 17 is the anniversary of the death of Patrick, the patron saint of Ireland, in the fourth century.
- According to legend, St. Patrick banished all the snakes from Ireland with the sound of a drum.

Bookmark # 9-21

SPECIFIC TIMES & DATES

Monday 22

April Fool's Day

- A more accurate name for April Fool's Day is "All Fools' Day."
- April Fool's Day may be a custom left over from the time when the New Year began on March 25 and April 1 marked the end of the weeklong celebration.
- Traditionally, April Fool's Day is a day people play practical jokes on each other or otherwise try to "fool" others.
- Someone who is tricked on April Fool's Day in France is known as "an April fish." People who still celebrated the New Year in April (after the calendar change) were called "April Fish." Some French people send each other chocolate "April Fish." In Scotland, someone who's been tricked is known as a "gowk" or "cuckoo."

Bookmark # 9-22

SPECIFIC TIMES & DATES

Monday 22

May Day

- May Day, celebrated on May 1, represents the rebirth of spring and new plants.
- In Elizabethan England, people celebrated May Day by dancing around a "Maypole" to give thanks to the goddess of agriculture and vegetation.
- Some people still follow the custom of giving others May baskets decorated with ribbons and spring flowers.

Bookmark # 9-23

SPECIFIC TIMES & DATES

Monday 22

V-E Day

At the end of World War II, German officials entered the headquarters of Allied Commander Dwight D. Eisenhower in Rheims, France. At 2:41 A.M. on May 7, 1945, the Germans signed a surrender that ended the war in Europe. This day is known as V-E Day, which stands for "Victory in Europe Day." The holiday is celebrated on May 8 at the request of General Eisenhower.

Bookmark # 9-24

SPECIFIC TIMES & DATES

Monday 22

Mother's Day

- Miss Anna M. Jarvis of Philadelphia organized a special church service to honor mothers in May 1907. The following year, other churches also honored mothers on a Sunday in May. In 1914, Mother's Day became an official holiday.
- Children often give their mothers cards and gifts, take them out to dinner, or do something else nice for them on Mother's Day.
- Traditionally on Mother's Day, people wear red carnations if their mothers are alive and white carnations if their mothers have passed away.

Bookmark # 9-25

SPECIFIC TIMES & DATES

Monday 22

Memorial Day

- May 30, 1868, was officially set aside for everyone to decorate the graves of Civil War soldiers and hold "fitting services" to honor them.
- Soon Memorial Day, also known as Decoration Day, became a day to honor all veterans, no matter when they served.
- The last Monday in May is now designated for people to honor all those who have died, especially those who served in the military. Flags are flown at half-staff to honor the veterans.

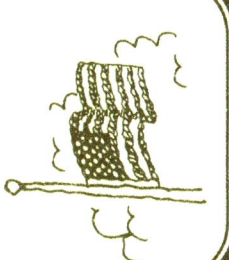

Bookmark # 9-26

SECTION II: Math, Times, and Specific Times and Dates | 25

Bookmark # 9-27

SPECIFIC TIMES & DATES
Monday 22

D Day

- "D Day" is the first day of a military plan of action.
- On June 6, 1944, thousands of American, British, Canadian, and other Allied troops stormed about 100 miles of beach along the French Normandy coast in an invasion of German-occupied territory. This surprise "D Day" attack changed the course of World War II. Less than a year later, Germany surrendered.

Bookmark # 9-28

SPECIFIC TIMES & DATES
Monday 22

Flag Day

- On June 14, 1777, the Continental Congress of Philadelphia officially adopted a design for the U.S. flag. The flag would "be of thirteen stripes of alternate red and white, with a union of thirteen stars of white in a blue field, representing the new constellation."
- The color blue represents a U.S. promise to work against oppression; the red color signifies daring; the white stands for purity.
- The first official flag was carried during the Battle of Brandywine on September 11, 1777.

Bookmark # 9-29

SPECIFIC TIMES & DATES
Monday 22

Father's Day

- In 1909, Mrs. John Bruce Dodd of Spokane, Washington, wrote to the Spokane Ministerial Association proposing the idea of honoring fathers. The first official Father's Day celebration occurred in 1910.
- Father's Day used to be celebrated on different days in different parts of the country. Starting in 1946, the third Sunday in June became the official national Father's Day.
- Traditionally on Father's Day, people wear red roses to honor their fathers who are alive and white roses to honor fathers who have passed away.

Bookmark # 9-30

SPECIFIC TIMES & DATES
Monday 22

Independence Day

- Independence Day honors the formal adoption of the Declaration of Independence on July 4, 1776, making the 13 colonies free of England's rule.
- Independence Day is now a popular day for picnics, parades, concerts, and fireworks.

Bookmark # 9-31

SPECIFIC TIMES & DATES
Monday 22

Labor Day

- Peter J. McGuire, president of the United Brotherhood of Carpenters and Joiners of America, first suggested Labor Day in 1882. He submitted a proposal to the Central Labor Union in New York asking for a day to represent the "great industrial spirit, the great vital force of the nation."
- Labor Day is often celebrated with fun activities as a break from laboring.

Veteran's Day

- Veteran's Day was first observed on November 11, 1919, to celebrate the end of World War I. The holiday, originally called Armistice Day, honored World War I veterans who "fought, and especially those who died" for peace.
- On November 11, 1921, the body of an unknown American soldier was buried in Arlington Cemetery.
- Armistice Day became an official holiday in 1938. The holiday's name was changed in 1954 to include all veterans.

Election Day

- In 1845, Congress passed an act declaring the first Tuesday after the first Monday in November the official day of elections in the United States, with the general presidential election held every four years.
- The 19th Amendment in 1920 gave women the right to vote.
- The 26th Amendment in 1971 gave 18-year-olds the right to vote. The age was lowered from 21 years.
- Voting in the United States is a volunteer activity. In some countries, people who don't vote are fined.

EXERCISE YOUR RIGHT TO VOTE!

Halloween

Halloween, or All Hallows Eve, dates back to Ancient England, where Druids celebrated the end of summer. They believed ghosts arrived with the darkness on this night. Now, traditional activities during Halloween festivals include dressing in costumes, lighting bonfires, making jack-o-lanterns, bobbing for apples, and trick-or-treating.

BOO

Columbus Day

- Columbus arrived in America on October 12, 1492, after a journey from Spain that lasted a little over two months.
- Columbus Day, now celebrated on the second Monday in October, is set aside to "provide an annual reaffirmation of the American people of their faith in the future, a declaration of willingness to face with confidence the imponderables of unknown tomorrows."
- Many people also celebrate the day as Indigenous Peoples Day to honor Native Americans, who were here before Columbus arrived.

Rosh Hashanah

- Rosh Hashanah is a holy Jewish holiday that is widely known as the Jewish New Year. It occurs in autumn, usually September, and is observed for two days.
- A shofar, or ram's horn, is blown to confuse Satan in his reporting. The horn also calls worshippers together and symbolizes the end of the High Holy Days on Yom Kippur, which occurs ten days after Rosh Hashanah.

Section II: Math, Times, and Specific Times and Dates | 27

Thanksgiving Day

Americans celebrated Thanksgiving for their land and crops as early as 1621. Early Thanksgiving celebrations began with a church service, then feasting. Food likely served at the first Thanksgiving feast included venison, duck, goose, seafood, bread, and vegetables—but not turkey. Dessert was probably wild plums and dried berries.

Bookmark # 9-37

Hanukkah

- Hanukkah, also known as the Festival of Lights, usually occurs in December, but sometimes begins in late November.
- Hanukkah has been celebrated by those of the Jewish faith since 165 B.C.
- Hanukkah celebrations last eight days. One candle in a menorah is lit each day as a reminder of a miracle in which a small amount of consecrated oil lasted eight days.

Bookmark # 9-38

Pearl Harbor Day

- On December 7, 1941, Japan surprised the U.S. forces with an attack at Hawaii's Pearl Harbor Navy Base. A soldier in Honolulu practicing with radar reported planes 132 miles away, but he was ignored.
- During the attack, more than 3,500 people were killed or wounded, eight battleships sunk, and six air bases damaged, as well as many cruisers and destroyers damaged or destroyed.
- President Franklin Roosevelt called the day a "date which will live in infamy." The United States declared war on Japan the following day.

Bookmark # 9-39

Christmas

- Christmas is the Christian celebration on December 25 of the birth of Jesus, although the exact date of Jesus' birth is not known.
- Christmas trees are from the tradition that some flowers and trees blossom only on Christmas.
- Santa Claus is derived from the German legend of St. Nicholas, who was probably born in what is now Turkey. He became a symbol of gift giving among Christians. Many countries have "Santa Claus" legends. His name probably comes from the Dutch "Sinter Klaas."
- Puritans in early New England outlawed celebrating Christmas.

Bookmark # 9-40

Kwanzaa

- Kwanzaa is a weeklong celebration of singing, dancing, and feasting from December 26 to January 1. A candle is lit on each day.
- Kwanzaa is based on African traditions devoted to family togetherness and the community. The name of the celebration means "first fruits" in Swahili.
- The Feast of Karamu is held at the end of the celebration. At this time, children receive gifts and elders are honored.

Bookmark # 9-41

28 | BOOKMARKS ACROSS THE CURRICULUM

Section III

History and Government

Boston Tea Party
HISTORY

Most early colonists in America drank a lot of tea. They became upset with the high taxes the British imposed on tea shipped to America. On December 16, 1773, colonists disguised themselves as Indians. They threw a British ship's cargo of tea overboard in Boston Harbor in protest of the taxes. The Boston Tea Party became a major event leading to the Revolutionary War.

Bookmark # 10-3

Industrial Revolution
HISTORY

Before the 1700s, most people in Europe lived and worked on farms. During the 1700s and early 1800s, many new machines were invented. Methods of manufacturing were improved. New means of transportation, such as railroads, were developed to move the goods produced in the factories. Factories needed more workers. At the same time, improvements in farm equipment required fewer people to operate a farm. People moved off the farms to work in factories. The time of all those changes is known as the Industrial Revolution.

Bookmark # 10-2

Creating Mummies
HISTORY

1. The internal organs were removed from the body (the brain was removed through the nose with a hook).
2. The organs were cleaned, dried, and individually wrapped, then placed back in the body.
3. Empty spots in the body were filled with sawdust, mud, tar, or linen.
4. The total body was wrapped in linen. The total length of the wrappings could be more than a mile and a half long.

Bookmark # 10-1

HISTORY

California Gold Rush

- In January 1848, near what is now Coloma, California, a carpenter named James Marshall found a nugget of gold near a sawmill owned by Captain John Sutter.
- President James Polk's speech to Congress mentioned the abundance of gold in California. This sparked the 1849 California Gold Rush.

Bookmark # 10-8

HISTORY

Valley Forge

- During the Revolutionary War, George Washington and his troops spent the winter of 1777 at Valley Forge, Pennsylvania. The 2,000 acres located along trade routes and near farm supplies seemed an ideal location.
- Troops cut down trees to make log cabins. Washington stayed in a drafty tent until all of his soldiers could be housed in cabins.
- The winter was unusually cold and snowy, and supplies were cut off. Nearly 2,500 of the 11,000 men died of starvation or disease during that winter.

Bookmark # 10-7

HISTORY

The U.S. Flag

- The Continental Congress passed a resolution for a flag on June 14, 1777.
- Although she did make flags, Betsy Ross likely didn't design the U.S. flag, as popular belief indicates. The flag may have been designed by Francis Hopkinson, one of the men who signed the Declaration of Independence.
- At first the U.S. flag kept the original 13 stars in a circle and added a new stripe for each state. Designers soon realized the space was too limited to keep adding stripes and added stars instead.

Bookmark # 10-6

HISTORY

Declaration of Independence

- Thomas Jefferson spent two weeks writing the original Declaration of Independence.
- The final document was signed by 56 men.
- Twelve of the colonies approved the Declaration of Independence. New York abstained from the vote, but ratified on July 9, 1776.
- The original Declaration of Independence is now located in the National Archives in Washington, DC.

Bookmark # 10-5

HISTORY

Intolerable Acts

- Boston Port Act—closed the city's harbor until payment for the ruined tea was made
- Massachusetts Government Act—took away the colony's charter
- Administration of Justice Act—allowed British officials to go to England or another colony for trial to protect them no matter what crime they committed
- Quartering Act—forced colonists to feed and house British soldiers
- Quebec Act—gave Quebec the right to the territory and fur trade between the Ohio and Mississippi Rivers

Bookmark # 10-4

HISTORY

The Emancipation Proclamation

- On September 22, 1862, President Abraham Lincoln told of his intention to free the slaves as a "fit and necessary war measure for suppressing said rebellion."

- On January 1, 1863, Lincoln issued the Emancipation Proclamation, freeing the slaves. The proclamation also asked that the slaves abstain from violence and "labor faithfully for reasonable wages." The Executive Government, including the military, would "recognize and maintain the freedom of said persons."

Bookmark # 10-13

HISTORY

Underground Railroad

- The Underground Railroad was neither underground nor a railroad. It was a path slaves took in the mid-1800s as they escaped the South to freedom in the North.

- Some people helped the slaves by hiding them during the day at places called "stations."

- Harriet Tubman, an escaped slave, is the most famous "conductor" on the Underground Railroad. She led more than 300 others to freedom.

- Thousands made the journey safely, although many were captured or killed.

Bookmark # 10-12

HISTORY

"Star Spangled Banner"

- On September 14, 1814, Francis Scott Key, while on a ship in the harbor, watched a battle between Americans and the British at Fort McHenry near Baltimore, Maryland.

- Seeing the American flag still flying over the fort at dawn inspired him to write a poem on the back of an envelope.

- The poem was set to music and became the official U.S. National Anthem on March 3, 1931.

Bookmark # 10-11

HISTORY

The Pony Express

In the mid-1800s, a letter often took three or four weeks or longer to go from Missouri to California—if the letter got there at all. In 1860, Senator William Gwin suggested moving mail by horseback, which would take only about 10 days. An advertisement went out asking for skinny expert riders not over 18 and, due to the dangers involved, said "orphans preferred." The Pony Express was used less than two years because the development of the telegraph made the service less needed.

Bookmark # 10-10

HISTORY

John Brown's Battle

- On the night of October 16, 1859, John Brown led 21 others into Harpers Ferry, Virginia, to capture an arsenal. He asked for the freedom of all slaves in the state.

- John Brown was found guilty of murder, treason, and rebellion. He was hanged for his crimes.

Bookmark # 10-9

SECTION III: History and Government

HISTORY

Civil War Uniforms

At first, Civil War soldiers didn't have specific uniforms. If they didn't wear their regular clothes, individual units wore whatever uniforms states, towns, companies, or individuals provided. Soldiers found it difficult to tell the enemy troops from their own and often opened fire on their own men. Eventually the Union Army adopted blue uniforms, and the Confederate Army adopted gray uniforms.

Bookmark # 10-14

HISTORY

Gettysburg Address

- President Lincoln delivered the Gettysburg Address while dedicating a national cemetery in Pennsylvania on November 19, 1863. His speech was to honor the men killed, wounded, or captured during the Battle of Gettysburg the previous July. The number of men was estimated to be 48,000 to 51,000.
- President Lincoln wrote the speech on the back of an envelope on the way to Gettysburg.
- Immediately after Lincoln gave the speech, most newspapers didn't think the speech was important enough to run on the front page.

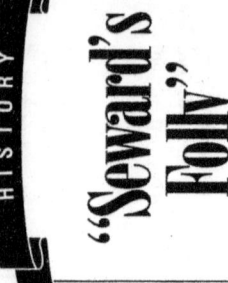

Bookmark # 10-15

HISTORY

Sherman's March to Atlanta

- In 1864, General William Tecumseh Sherman and his army of 60,000 soldiers marched their way across Georgia. Wherever they went, they took whatever food, weapons, clothes, and valuables they wanted. What they didn't steal, they destroyed.
- In December, Sherman and his troops burned 4,100 of Atlanta's 4,500 buildings, severely cutting off supplies to the Confederate Army.
- While Atlanta burned, Sherman sent a cable to the War Department saying, "Atlanta is ours, and fairly won."

Bookmark # 10-16

HISTORY

End of the Civil War

- In 1865, tired and hungry Confederate troops arrived in Appomattox, Virginia. Many had worn their boots completely through after marching 90 miles in six days.
- On April 9, 1865, General Robert E. Lee surrendered to General Ulysses S. Grant in the courthouse at Appomattox, thereby ending the Civil War. Grant said, "Our conversation grew so pleasant . . ."
- Grant gave orders to make sure the Confederate soldiers were fed, then allowed them to return to their homes instead of putting them in prison.

Bookmark # 10-17

HISTORY

"Seward's Folly"

- In 1867, William H. Seward, U.S. Secretary of State, noticed Russia's financial difficulties. He purchased Alaska from the Russians for $7,200,000, or about 2 cents per acre.
- Many people thought Seward's purchase was foolish and called the area "Seward's Folly" or "Icebergia." Natives of the area called the place *Alakshah*, meaning "great country."
- People eventually realized that Alaska was one of the best investments the United States ever made when gold and then oil were discovered.

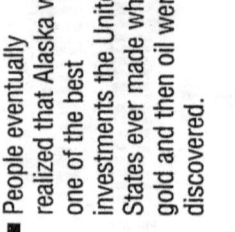

Bookmark # 10-18

Transcontinental Railroad

HISTORY

- Workers on the Transcontinental Railroad had many problems, including bad weather, flea and lice infestations, attacks from Native American tribes defending their land, and prejudice toward the Chinese- and Irish-American workers.

- Workers started from each city. The last connecting rails of the Transcontinental Railroad were laid near Promontory Point, Utah, on May 10, 1869.

Bookmark # 10-19

The Great Chicago Fire

HISTORY

On October 8, 1871, a fire started in the O'Learys' barn in Chicago. One legend is that a cow kicked over a lantern. The fire quickly spread through the surrounding buildings and wooden sidewalks. The fire lasted 27 hours and burned more than 17,000 buildings. About 300 people died, hundreds more were injured, and thousands were left homeless.

Bookmark # 10-20

Little Big Horn

HISTORY

- The national government had promised that the Black Hills of South Dakota would belong to Native Americans forever— until gold was discovered in the area in the 1870s. Then white men set up mining operations on sacred land.

- The Native Americans fought for their land. On June 25, 1876, Crazy Horse and his men surrounded General George Armstrong Custer and his troops, who were greatly outnumbered. Within 30 minutes, every white man at the Battle of Little Big Horn was killed.

Bookmark # 10-21

Ellis Island

HISTORY

- More than 15 million people passed through the immigration station on Ellis Island in New York Harbor between 1892 and 1954.

- Immigrants spent two or three weeks crossing the Atlantic Ocean. After the ship docked, passengers left in order of those who paid the most for their trip.

- Immigrants had to pass physical examinations, then tell whether they could read or write, and how they'd earn a living in America. Between 200,000 and 300,000 people failed to pass the admission test and had to return to their native land.

Bookmark # 10-22

The Great Depression

HISTORY

After the stock marked collapsed on October 24, 1929, individuals and businesses, including banks, lost their money. Many people were unemployed and little money was available. During the Depression in the 1930s, the weather, with drought, floods, windstorms, and other problems, added to people's suffering. Conditions improved when the start of World War II gave people jobs supplying the military.

Bookmark # 10-23

SECTION III: History and Government | 33

HISTORY

Attack on Pearl Harbor

- On December 7, 1941, Japanese bombers sunk or heavily damaged 18 of 96 ships in Pearl Harbor near Honolulu, Hawaii.
- During the two-hour attack, 2,400 people were killed and 1,178 people were wounded.
- After the attack on Pearl Harbor, the United States became fully involved in World War II.

Bookmark # 10-24

HISTORY

Japanese Relocation Camps

- On March 18, 1942, President Franklin Roosevelt issued the War Relocation Authority, which forced people of Japanese ancestry to live in relocation camps.
- Many of these camps were in barns with linoleum to cover the manure that hadn't been cleaned.
- Each family was given a space about 20 feet square. They had little privacy from other families.
- In 1989, the government gave $20,000 to each Japanese-American who had been forced to stay in a relocation camp.

Bookmark # 10-25

HISTORY

Watergate

- On June 17, 1972, police discovered five people with spy equipment breaking into the offices at the Watergate building in Washington, DC. The offices were the headquarters of the Democratic National Committee.
- After he was re-elected, President Richard Nixon, who was Republican, was discovered to have been involved in the break-in; he had denied knowledge of the spying operation.
- Nixon resigned from office on August 9, 1974, before he could be impeached.

Bookmark # 10-26

GOVERNMENT

Types of Government

- Democracy—the government is run by the people through representatives elected by popular vote
- Dependency—the government is ruled by another country; the land is geographically distinct from the country governing it
- Federal State—the power is divided between a central government and several regional governments
- Monarchy—the head of the government is a king or queen; sometimes much of the power is delegated to others
- Republic—the head of state is an elected president who is trusted to do the will of the people
- Socialism—everyone in the society shares equally

Bookmark # 11-1

GOVERNMENT

The U.S. Constitution

- In 1787, states chose 79 men to attend the Constitutional Convention at the State House, later called Independence Hall, in Philadelphia.
- The 55 men who attended the convention, with George Washington leading the proceedings, spent four months working on a document that outlined the basic rules of how people would govern themselves and protect their liberty.
- The document, which came to be known as the Constitution, was signed on September 17, 1787.

Bookmark # 11-2

34 | BOOKMARKS ACROSS THE CURRICULUM

GOVERNMENT

PROCESS OF MAKING LAWS IN CONGRESS

1. A senator or representative proposes a bill, which is a written statement of a possible future law.
2. Committees consider the bill and may make changes.
3. Members of Congress discuss the bill.
4. Congress votes on the bill.
5. If the bill is approved, the president either signs it into law or vetoes it.

Bookmark # 11-7

GOVERNMENT

U.S. PRESIDENT

To be eligible to be a U.S. president, a person must

- be a natural-born citizen, which means someone who is a U.S. citizen at birth, not one who becomes a citizen later in life (this rule didn't apply in the early years of the country, when many adults were immigrants)
- be at least 35 years old
- have lived in the United States at least 14 years
- have served less than two four-year terms as president (Franklin Roosevelt was president 11 years, longer than any other president)

Bookmark # 11-6

GOVERNMENT

THE REPUBLICAN PARTY

- The Republican Party began on July 6, 1854, on the principle of abolishing slavery.
- The first Republican National Convention took place in Philadelphia on June 17, 1856. Their candidate for president, Colonel John C. Fremont, lost the election to Democrat James Buchanan.
- The symbol for the Republican Party is an elephant.

Bookmark # 11-5

GOVERNMENT

THE DEMOCRATIC PARTY

- The origin of the Democratic Party was the Democratic-Republican Party, led by Thomas Jefferson.
- The Democratic Party has its basis in helping "the common person" and wants the federal government to support social and economic programs.
- The symbol for the Democratic Party is a donkey.

Bookmark # 11-4

GOVERNMENT

THE BILL OF RIGHTS

The first 10 amendments to the United States Constitution are known as the Bill of Rights. Some of the provisions of the Bill of Rights are

- freedom of speech
- freedom of religion
- the right to peaceful gatherings
- the right to keep and bear arms
- the right to be free of illegal search and seizures
- the right of a person not to incriminate himself or herself
- the right to a speedy trial by an impartial jury
- freedom from "cruel and unusual punishment"

Bookmark # 11-3

SECTION III: *History and Government* | 35

GOVERNMENT

CENSUS

- Every 10 years, the U.S. government counts the people who live in the country. The census takers gather information on the ages of people, where they live, what they do for a living, how much money they earn, and more.

- The information is valuable. For example, knowing how many children are in an area can help plan future schools.

- The first census was taken in 1790. At that time, about 3,929,000 people lived in the United States. By 2000, that number had grown to 281,421,906.

Bookmark # 11-9

GOVERNMENT

THE SUPREME COURT

- The Supreme Court's purpose is to interpret the U.S. Constitution to make sure everyone is treated fairly. The Supreme Court is the highest ruling body in the United States; not even the president has more power.

- The nine Supreme Court justices are appointed by the president. At one time, the Supreme Court had only six justices.

- The Supreme Court has been located in New York City, Philadelphia, and the Capitol in Washington, DC. Since 1935, the judges have met in the Supreme Court Building in Washington, DC.

Bookmark # 11-8

SECTION IV

Geography and Famous Places

THE SEVEN CONTINENTS

- Africa—second largest continent
- Antarctica—continent at the bottom of the world; has no permanent population because the land is covered in ice
- Asia—largest continent in both population and landmass
- Australia—smallest continent in area
- Europe—second smallest continent in area
- North America—continent containing the United States
- South America—continent connected to North America by a strip of land called Central America

Bookmark # 12-1

AFRICA

- Africa has 53 countries, more than any other continent.
- The climate of Africa varies greatly. Some areas get 100 or more inches of rain a year, while other areas may not receive a significant rainfall for several years.
- Some areas of Africa are totally modern, while others are still largely primitive.
- More than 1,000 different languages are spoken in Africa.

Bookmark # 12-2

ANTARCTICA

- Antarctica, located at the bottom of the world, is covered in ice up to three miles thick. Few plants and animals are able to exist in its environment. Antarctica may be without sunlight for months at a time, and temperatures often drop to 100 degrees below zero.
- No countries exist in Antarctica, but many scientists spend time there to study the environment and search for any natural resources it may contain.
- Some people want to make Antarctica a world park.

Bookmark # 12-3

SECTION IV: GEOGRAPHY AND FAMOUS PLACES | 37

THE CONTINENTS

ASIA

- Asia contains nearly one-third of Earth's total land area.
- Both the world's highest mountain (Mount Everest) and the world's lowest point (Shore of the Dead Sea) are located in Asia.
- Asia is home to some of the world's most densely populated areas, such as China and Japan, as well as one of the most sparsely populated areas, Siberia.
- Much of Asia was conquered by Europeans, although many countries have since become independent nations.

Bookmark # 12-4

AUSTRALIA

- Map makers in the 1600s thought a landmass was likely in the location of what is now Australia. They called it *Terra Australis Incognita*, meaning "The Unknown Land of the South."
- The continent of Australia, including the island of Tasmania, is about the same size as the continental United States.
- Many island groups in the Pacific Ocean are considered part of the continent of Australia.

Bookmark # 12-5

EUROPE

- Because Europe and Asia are connected, many people consider them to be only one continent called Eurasia. Europe is actually a large peninsula of the continent of Asia. The Caucasus and Ural mountains form the boundary between the two continents.
- By the 1700s, Europeans had colonized, and therefore ruled, much of the world. Many of their colonies, such as the United States, are now independent.
- Both World War I and World War II began in Europe.

Bookmark # 12-6

NORTH AMERICA

- The northern part of North America extends to the frozen tundra above the Arctic Circle, while the southern part of North America supports tropical rain forests.
- Europeans once ruled all of the 23 countries in North America. Although most North American countries are now independent, several still have strong European influences.

Bookmark # 12-7

SOUTH AMERICA

- South America contains many natural resources, but often the environment is greatly damaged to get those resources.
- South America has nearly twice the square miles as Europe, whose people once conquered much of the larger continent.
- Spanish is the primary language in each of the 12 independent countries of South America except where Portuguese is spoken.

Bookmark # 12-8

BOOKMARKS ACROSS THE CURRICULUM

COUNTRIES

Largest Countries

The largest countries by area, in order, are

- Russia
- Canada
- China
- United States
- Brazil
- Australia
- India
- Kazakhstan
- Sudan

The largest countries by population, in order, are

- China
- India
- United States
- Indonesia
- Brazil
- Russia
- Pakistan
- Japan
- Nigeria

Bookmark # 13-1

COUNTRIES

Australia

- Australia is the only country that is also a continent.
- Because the continent of Australia is in the Southern Hemisphere, winter occurs while the United States is experiencing summer and vice versa. Also, daytime in the United States is nighttime in Australia.
- The first English settlement was a penal colony at Sydney Cove, established in 1787.

Bookmark # 13-2

COUNTRIES

Brazil

- Early explorers to Brazil took a type of wood that produced a red dye back to their home countries. This wood, called *pau-brasil*, gave the country its name.
- Brazil is South America's largest nation. The country consists of nearly half of South America's land.
- Brazil borders every nation on the South American continent except Chile and Ecuador.

Bookmark # 13-3

COUNTRIES

Burkina Faso

- Burkina Faso, in West Africa, is one of the three poorest countries in the world.
- Until 1984, Burkina Faso was called Upper Volta. The new name, meaning "the land of upright men," combines terms from two of the nation's languages.
- Fewer than 20% of the people in Burkina Faso can read and write.
- One of Burkina Faso's major exports is people! Many people leave the country to find work in neighboring countries, such as the Ivory Coast.

Bookmark # 13-4

COUNTRIES

Canada

- Canada, with its 13 provinces and territories, is second only to Russia as the largest country in the world.
- Canada contains more pine and spruce trees than any other country in the world.
- Most Canadian cities are in the southern part, where temperatures are warmer.
- The International Peace Garden, located on the border between North Dakota and Manitoba, Canada, is a promise that the two countries will remain friendly.

Bookmark # 13-5

SECTION IV: GEOGRAPHY AND FAMOUS PLACES 39

COUNTRIES

Chile

- Chile is 10 times longer than it is wide. The country stretches 2,647 miles north to south. The average width is only 110 miles. Its widest point east to west is 248 miles.
- About one-third of Chile is covered by the Andes Mountains.
- The Atacama Desert, the driest place on Earth, is located in the northern part of Chile.
- Chile, Argentina, and the United Kingdom claim power over nearly 500,000 square miles of Antarctic territory.

Bookmark # 13-6

China

- China is slightly larger in size than the United States.
- Work on the Great Wall of China began about 2,200 years ago to help protect the country from invasion from the West. The Great Wall cannot be seen from the Moon, as some people believe.
- The official religion of China is atheist, but the traditional religion follows some of the teachings of Confucius and Buddha.

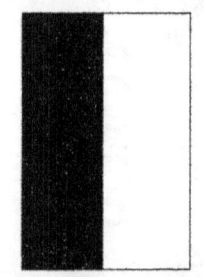

Bookmark # 13-7

Egypt

- Egypt is about 50% larger than Texas. The land, divided by the Nile River, is very dry.
- The 100-mile-long Suez Canal in Egypt connects the Red Sea and the Mediterranean Sea.
- Egyptian history dates back about 5,000 years. One of Egypt's most famous persons was Cleopatra.
- About half the people of Egypt are able to read and write.

Bookmark # 13-8

Indonesia

- Indonesia consists of about 17,000 islands. Only about 11,000 of the islands have people living on them. The largest islands are Sumatra, Java, Bali, Kalimantan, and Celebes (also known as Sulawesi).
- Indonesia has 20% of the active volcanoes in the world, and earthquakes are frequent.
- Indonesia is divided by the "Wallace Line." Plant and animal life are more similar to that of Asia on one side and more similar to Australia on the other side.

Bookmark # 13-9

Japan

- The entire landmass of Japan consists of several islands. The area of Japan (377,837 sq. km or 145,884 sq. mi.) is about the same as the area of Montana (380,847 sq. km or 147,046 sq. mi.).
- The four main islands are Honshu, Hokkaido, Kyushu, and Shikoku.
- Japan has about 1,500 earthquakes a year. Most are minor. Much of the destruction from earthquakes is caused by tsunamis, which are gigantic ocean waves caused by earthquakes under the ocean.

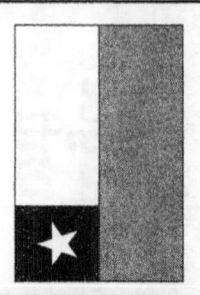

Bookmark # 13-10

40 | BOOKMARKS ACROSS THE CURRICULUM

★ STATES ★

States

- Washington, DC, the capital of the 50 United States, isn't located in any state, but is a separate area.
- The 50 states became states on 49 different days. Only North Dakota and South Dakota became states on the same day. North Dakota is considered to have become a state before South Dakota because *N* comes before *S* alphabetically.
- In landmass, Alaska is the largest state, and Rhode Island is the smallest.
- Alaska is the state located farthest north, and Hawaii is the state located farthest south.

★
★ ★
★ ★

Bookmark # 14-1

COUNTRIES

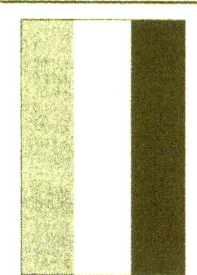

Vatican City

- The entire country of Vatican City is located on 109 acres, less than a square mile, within the city of Rome. Vatican City is the only survivor of the Papal States that consisted of about 17,000 square miles as recently as 1870.
- The population of Vatican City is estimated at fewer than 1,000 people. Many are dignitaries, priests, nuns, and guards. The pope, who gains lifetime rule after being appointed, has complete executive and judicial power over Vatican City.

Bookmark # 13-14

COUNTRIES

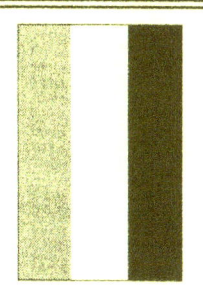

Thailand

- Thailand is shaped similar to an elephant's head, part of the reason the elephant is the national symbol of Thailand. Elephants are also used as beasts of burden in the country.
- Until 1939, Thailand was called Siam. Siamese cats, which are native to Thailand, get their name from the country.

Bookmark # 13-13

COUNTRIES

South Africa

- In 1652, Dutch settlers called the native South African people "stammerers" because their language sounded strange to the Europeans. Influenced by the Dutch language, a dialect known as Afrikaans developed.
- After an abundance of diamonds in South Africa was discovered in 1867 and gold in 1886, many people from other nations traveled to the area in the hope of becoming rich.
- Repeal of the apartheid laws in 1991 is slowly improving race relations in South Africa.

Bookmark # 13-12

COUNTRIES

The Netherlands

- The Netherlands is also known as Holland and is part of the Low Countries with Belgium and Luxembourg.
- About half of the land in the Netherlands is located below sea level. Dikes are necessary to control the flow of water and keep the land usable.
- The Netherlands is known for tulips, wooden shoes, and windmills.

Bookmark # 13-11

SECTION IV: GEOGRAPHY AND FAMOUS PLACES 41

★ ★ STATES ★ ★
Alabama

Became the 22nd state on December 14, 1819

Nickname—Yellowhammer State

Motto—We dare defend our rights

Capital—Montgomery

State Bird—yellowhammer

State Flower—camellia

Postal Abbreviation—AL

Fun Facts:
- The Confederacy was founded at Montgomery in February 1861.
- Many civil rights events, such as the 1965 Freedom March and the bus boycott in 1955-56, took place in Alabama.

★ ★ STATES ★ ★
Alaska

Became the 49th state on January 3, 1959

Nicknames—The Last Frontier and Land of the Midnight Sun

Motto—North to the Future

Capital—Juneau

State Bird—willow ptarmigan

State Flower—forget-me-not

Postal Abbreviation—AK

Fun Facts:
- Alaska is about one-fifth the size of the continental United States.
- Alaska's population consists of about 75.7% white residents. Eskimo, Aleut and other natives make up about 15.7%.

★ ★ STATES ★ ★
Arizona

Became the 48th state on February 14, 1912

Nickname—Grand Canyon State

Motto—God enriches

Capital—Phoenix

State Bird—cactus wren

State Flower—saguaro (giant cactus)

Postal Abbreviation—AZ

Fun Facts:
- Arizona is home to at least 14 Native American tribes.
- The gunfight at O.K. Corral took place in Tombstone, Arizona.
- Some Arizona attractions are the Grand Canyon, Hoover Dam, the Painted Desert, and the Petrified Forest.

★ ★ STATES ★ ★
Arkansas

Became the 25th state on June 15, 1836

Nickname—Land of Opportunity

Motto—The people rule

Capital—Little Rock

State Bird—mockingbird

State Flower—apple blossom

Postal Abbreviation—AR

Fun Facts:
- Arkansas has the only diamond mine located in the United States.
- During the Civil War, Arkansas was part of the Confederacy, but Union troops occupied the northern part of the state.

★ ★ STATES ★ ★
California

Became the 31st state on September 9, 1850

Nickname—Golden State

Motto—Eureka (I have found it)

Capital—Sacramento

State Bird—California valley quail

State Flower—golden poppy

Postal Abbreviation—CA

Fun Facts:
- Death Valley, at 282 feet below sea level, is the lowest place in the continental United States.
- California is home to Disneyland, the Golden Gate Bridge, and Yosemite National Park.

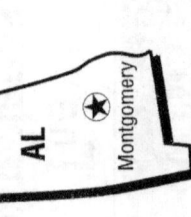

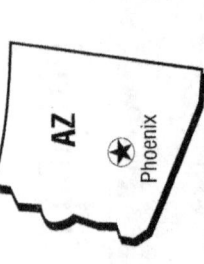

★ STATES ★ Colorado

Became the 38th state on August 1, 1876

Nickname—Centennial State

Motto—Nothing without Providence

Capital—Denver

State Bird—lark bunting

State Flower—Rocky Mountain columbine

Postal Abbreviation—CO

Fun Facts:
- Colorado's name comes from a Spanish word meaning "red" or "ruddy."
- Over 1,000 mountain peaks in Colorado are more than 10,000 feet high.

CO ★ Denver

Bookmark # 14-7

★ STATES ★ Connecticut

Became the 5th state on January 9, 1788

Nicknames—Constitution State and Nutmeg State

Motto—He who transplanted still sustains

Capital—Hartford

State Bird—robin

State Flower—mountain laurel

Postal Abbreviation—CT

Fun Facts:
- Connecticut served as the Continental Army's major supplier during the Revolutionary War, and was known as the "Provisions State."
- The oldest U.S. newspaper still in existence is the *Hartford Courant*, which started in 1764.

CT ★ Hartford

Bookmark # 14-8

★ STATES ★ Delaware

Became the 1st state on December 7, 1787

Nicknames—First State, Diamond State, and Small Wonder

Motto—Liberty and independence

Capital—Dover

State Bird—blue hen chicken

State Flower—peach blossom

Postal Abbreviation—DE

Fun Facts:
- Henry Hudson discovered Delaware in 1609.
- Delaware was a slave state during the Civil War, but did not secede from the Union.

DE ★ Dover

Bookmark # 14-9

★ STATES ★ Florida

Became the 27th state on March 3, 1845

Nickname—Sunshine State

Motto—In God we trust

Capital—Tallahassee

State Bird—mockingbird

State Flower—orange blossom

Postal Abbreviation—FL

Fun Facts:
- St. Augustine, established in 1565, is the oldest permanent city in the United States.
- Attractions in Florida include Disney World, Epcot Center, the Everglades, and the Kennedy Space Center.

★ Tallahassee FL

Bookmark # 14-10

★ STATES ★ Georgia

Became the 4th state on January 2, 1788

Nicknames—Empire State of the South and Peach State

Motto—Wisdom, justice, and moderation

Capital—Atlanta

State Bird—brown thrasher

State Flower—Cherokee rose

Postal Abbreviation—GA

Fun Facts:
- The first Europeans who settled in Georgia were people who owed a lot of money in England.
- The images of three Confederate generals are carved in the side of Stone Mountain, a huge granite block.

GA ★ Atlanta

Bookmark # 14-11

SECTION IV: GEOGRAPHY AND FAMOUS PLACES | 43

★ ★ STATES ★ ★

Hawaii
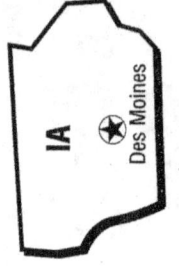

Became the 50th state on August 21, 1959

Nickname—Aloha State

Motto—The life of the land is perpetuated in righteousness

Capital—Honolulu

State Bird—nene (Hawaiian goose)

State Flower—hibiscus

Postal Abbreviation—HI

Fun Facts:
- Captain James Cook discovered the Hawaiian Islands in 1778. He called them the Sandwich Islands.
- Mauna Loa is one of the largest volcanic mountains in the world.

Bookmark # 14-12

★ ★ STATES ★ ★

Idaho

Became the 43rd state on July 3, 1890

Nickname—Gem State

Motto—It is forever

Capital—Boise

State Bird—mountain bluebird

State Flower—syringa

Postal Abbreviation—ID

Fun Facts:
- Several theories exist as to the origin of the word *Idaho*. *Idaho* may be a made-up name with no known meaning, or it may mean "gem of the mountains." Another source suggests that *Idaho* may be a Kiowa Apache term for the Comanche.
- Idaho is known for its potatoes. The state produces about one-fourth of the potatoes in the United States.
- The largest elk herds in the United States can be found in Idaho.

Bookmark # 14-13

★ ★ STATES ★ ★

Illinois

Became the 21st state on December 3, 1818

Nickname—Land of Lincoln and Prairie State

Motto—State sovereignty, national union

Capital—Springfield

State Bird—cardinal

State Flower—native violet

Postal Abbreviation—IL

Fun Facts:
- Illinois gets its name from the Algonquin word for "tribe of superior men."
- The opening of the Erie Canal in 1825 brought many settlers to the Northwest Territory.

IL ★ Springfield

Bookmark # 14-14

★ ★ STATES ★ ★

Indiana
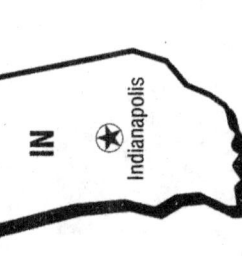

Became the 19th state on December 11, 1816

Nickname—Hoosier State

Motto—The Crossroads of America

Capital—Indianapolis

State Bird—cardinal

State Flower—peony

Postal Abbreviation—IN

Fun Facts:
- Indiana is a major producer of limestone and coal.
- Attractions in Indiana include Indianapolis Motor Speedway, Lincoln Boyhood National Memorial, and Wyandotte Cave.

IN ★ Indianapolis

Bookmark # 14-15

★ ★ STATES ★ ★

Iowa
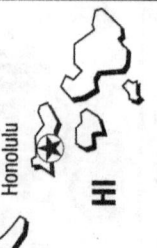

Became the 29th state on December 28, 1846

Nickname—Hawkeye State

Motto—Our liberties we prize and our rights we will maintain

Capital—Des Moines

State Bird—eastern goldfinch

State Flower—wild rose

Postal Abbreviation—IA

Fun Facts:
- Iowa's name comes from the Native American word for "the beautiful land."

IA ★ Des Moines

Bookmark # 14-16

---

44 | BOOKMARKS ACROSS THE CURRICULUM

★ ★ STATES ★ ★
Kansas

Became the 34th state on January 29, 1861

Nicknames—Jayhawk State and Sunflower State

Motto—To the stars through difficulties

Capital—Topeka

State Bird—western meadowlark

State Flower—native sunflower

Postal Abbreviation—KS

Fun Facts:
- Fort Leavenworth, Fort Riley, Fort Larned, and Fort Scott were founded to protect travelers along the Santa Fe and Oregon Trails.
- Kansas is the leading producer of winter wheat and helium in the United States.

KS ★ Topeka

Bookmark # 14-17

★ ★ STATES ★ ★
Kentucky

Became the 15th state on June 1, 1792

Nickname—Bluegrass State

Motto—United we stand, divided we fall

Capital—Frankfort

State Bird—Kentucky cardinal

State Flower—goldenrod

Postal Abbreviation—KY

Fun Facts:
- Kentucky was the first area west of the Allegheny Mountains that pioneers settled.
- During the Civil War, Kentucky had many supporters for both the Union and the Confederacy.

★ Frankfort
KY

Bookmark # 14-18

★ ★ STATES ★ ★
Louisiana

Became the 18th state on April 30, 1812

Nickname—Pelican State

Motto—Union, justice, and confidence

Capital—Baton Rouge

State Bird—brown pelican

State Flower—magnolia

Postal Abbreviation—LA

Fun Facts:
- American troops defeated the British Army at the Battle of New Orleans. Neither side knew the War of 1812 was officially over by then.

★ Baton Rouge
LA

Bookmark # 14-19

★ ★ STATES ★ ★
Maine

Became the 23rd state on March 15, 1820

Nickname—Pine Tree State

Motto—I lead

Capital—Augusta

State Bird—chickadee

State Flower—white pine cone and tassel

Postal Abbreviation—ME

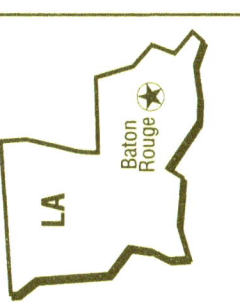

ME
★ Augusta

Bookmark # 14-20

★ ★ STATES ★ ★
Maryland

Became the 7th state on April 28, 1788

Nicknames—Free State and Old Line State

Motto—Manly deeds, womanly words

Capital—Annapolis

State Bird—Baltimore oriole

State Flower—black-eyed Susan

Postal Abbreviation—MD

Fun Facts:
- During the Civil War, Maryland was a slave state, but didn't secede from the Union.
- Chesapeake Bay produces more seafood than any other similar body of water.
- Maryland's name comes from Queen Henrietta Maria, wife of Charles I of England.
- Maryland is the largest producer of cranberries in the United States.

Bookmark # 14-21

SECTION IV: GEOGRAPHY AND FAMOUS PLACES | 45

★ STATES ★
Missouri

Became the 24th state on August 10, 1821

Nickname—Show-Me State

Motto—The welfare of the people shall be the supreme law

Capital—Jefferson City

State Bird—bluebird

State Flower—hawthorn

Postal Abbreviation—MO

Fun Facts:
- The Gateway Arch in St. Louis symbolizes Missouri's importance in settling the West.
- About 90% of the U.S. lead supply comes from Missouri.

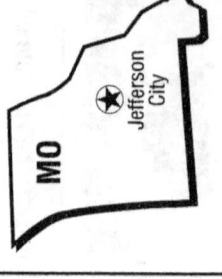
MO — Jefferson City

Bookmark # 14-26

★ STATES ★
Mississippi

Became the 20th state on December 10, 1817

Nickname—Magnolia State

Motto—By valor and arms

Capital—Jackson

State Bird—mockingbird

State Flower—magnolia

Postal Abbreviation—MS

Fun Facts:
- Mississippi's name is from a Native American word meaning "Father of Waters," "great river," or "gathering-in of all the waters."
- More pond-raised catfish come from Mississippi than anywhere else in the world.

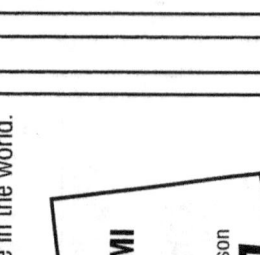
MI — Jackson

Bookmark # 14-25

★ STATES ★
Minnesota

Became the 32nd state on May 11, 1858

Nicknames—Gopher State, Land of 10,000 Lakes, and North Star State

Motto—The North Star

Capital—St. Paul

State Bird—common loon

State Flower—pink-and-white lady's slipper

Postal Abbreviation—MN

Fun Facts:
- Minnesota is the leading producer of iron ore in the United States.
- Minnesota is home to the Guthrie Theatre, the Mall of America, and the Mayo Clinic.

MN — St. Paul

Bookmark # 14-24

★ STATES ★
Michigan

Became the 26th state on January 26, 1837

Nickname—Wolverine State

Motto—If you seek a pleasant peninsula, look around you

Capital—Lansing

State Bird—robin

State Flower—apple blossom

Postal Abbreviation—MI

Fun Facts:
- The state of Michigan is divided into upper and lower peninsulas.
- Four of the five Great Lakes have shores in Michigan.
- Michigan is the U.S. leader in the production of motor vehicles.

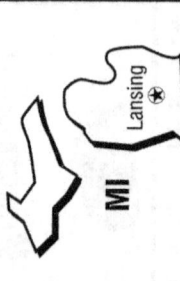
MI — Lansing

Bookmark # 14-23

★ STATES ★
Massachusetts

Became the 6th state on February 6, 1788

Nicknames—Bay State and Old Colony State

Motto—By the sword we seek peace, but peace only under liberty

Capital—Boston

State Bird—chickadee

State Flower—mayflower

Postal Abbreviation—MA

MA — Boston

Bookmark # 14-22

★ STATES ★
New Jersey

Became the 3rd state on December 18, 1787

Nickname—Garden State

Motto—Liberty and prosperity

Capital—Trenton

State Bird—eastern goldfinch

State Flower—purple violet

Postal Abbreviation—NJ

Fun Facts:
- Many battles took place in New Jersey during the American Revolution.
- New Jersey is a primary research center for the chemical industry.

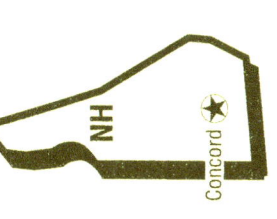

Bookmark # 14-31

★ STATES ★
New Hampshire

Became the 9th state on June 21, 1788

Nickname—Granite State

Motto—Live free or die

Capital—Concord

State Bird—purple finch

State Flower—purple lilac

Postal Abbreviation—NH

Fun Facts:
- New Hampshire is named for the county of Hampshire in England.

Bookmark # 14-30

★ STATES ★
Nevada

Became the 36th state on October 31, 1864

Nicknames—Battle Born State, Sagebrush State, and Silver State

Motto—All for Our Country

Capital—Carson City

State Bird—mountain bluebird

State Flower—sagebrush

Postal Abbreviation—NV

Fun Facts:
- Nevada has an annual rainfall of only nine inches, making it the driest state in the nation.
- The Comstock Lode in Nevada has the largest silver deposit in the United States.

Bookmark # 14-29

★ STATES ★
Nebraska

Became the 37th state on March 1, 1867

Nicknames—Beef State and Cornhusker State

Motto—Equality before the law

Capital—Lincoln

State Bird—western meadowlark

State Flower—Goldenrod

Postal Abbreviation—NE

Bookmark # 14-28

★ STATES ★
Montana

Became the 41st state on November 8, 1889

Nickname—Treasure State

Motto—Gold and silver

Capital—Helena

State Bird—western meadowlark

State Flower—bitterroot

Postal Abbreviation—MT

Fun Facts:
- Montana's name comes from a combination of Spanish and Latin words meaning "mountainous."
- Montana's attractions include Glacier and Yellowstone National Parks and Little Bighorn Battlefield.

Bookmark # 14-27

SECTION IV: GEOGRAPHY AND FAMOUS PLACES

★ STATES ★
New Mexico

Became the 47th state on January 6, 1912
Nickname—Land of Enchantment
Motto—It grows as it goes
Capital—Santa Fe
State Bird—roadrunner
State Flower—yucca flower
Postal Abbreviation—NM

Fun Facts:
- New Mexico is known for its energy research.
- New Mexico is home to Carlsbad Caverns and Roswell, the supposed crash landing site of a UFO in 1947.

Bookmark # 14-32

★ STATES ★
New York

Became the 11th state on July 26, 1788
Nickname—Empire State
Motto—Ever upward
Capital—Albany
State Bird—bluebird
State Flower—rose
Postal Abbreviation—NY

Fun Facts:
- New York is named in honor of the Duke of York.
- According to legend, Peter Minuit bought Manhattan Island for about $24 worth of trinkets.
- New York City was the U.S. capital until the administration of John Adams.

Bookmark # 14-33

★ STATES ★
North Carolina

Became the 12th state on November 21, 1789
Nickname—Tar Heel State
Motto—To be rather than to seem
Capital—Raleigh
State Bird—cardinal
State Flower—flowering dogwood
Postal Abbreviation—NC

Fun Facts:
- In 1587, Virginia Dare of North Carolina became the first baby born to English parents in America.
- North Carolina produces the most brick, furniture, textiles, and tobacco in the country.

Bookmark # 14-34

★ STATES ★
North Dakota

Became the 39th state on November 2, 1889
Nicknames—Flickertail State, Peace Garden State, Rough Rider State, and Sioux State
Motto—Liberty and union, now and forever: one and inseparable
Capital—Bismarck
State Bird—western meadowlark
State Flower—wild prairie rose
Postal Abbreviation—ND

Fun Facts:
- More than 90% of North Dakota is rural.
- The geographical center of North America is near Rugby, North Dakota.

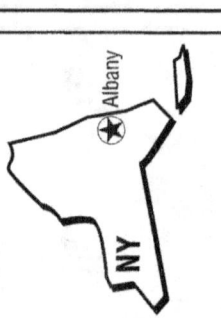

Bookmark # 14-35

★ STATES ★
Ohio

Became the 17th state on March 1, 1803
Nickname—Buckeye State
Motto—With God all things are possible
Capital—Columbus
State Bird—cardinal
State Flower—scarlet carnation
Postal Abbreviation—OH

Fun Facts:
- Ohio's name comes from an Iroquois word meaning "great river."
- Ohio is the nation's leading producer of lime.
- Attractions in Ohio include the Pro Football Hall of Fame and the Rock and Roll Hall of Fame and Museum.

Bookmark # 14-36

★ STATES ★

Oklahoma

Became the 46th state on November 16, 1907

Nickname—Sooner State

Motto—Labor conquers all things

Capital—Oklahoma City

State Bird—scissor-tailed flycatcher

State Flower—mistletoe

Postal Abbreviation—OK

Fun Facts:
- April 22, 1889, was the first day homesteading was allowed in Oklahoma. People who tried to beat the starting time were called "Sooners."
- Oklahoma is rich in oil and natural gas deposits.

OK ★ Oklahoma City

Bookmark # 14-37

★ STATES ★

Oregon

Became the 33rd state on February 14, 1859

Nickname—Beaver State

Motto—She flies with her own wings

Capital—Salem

State Bird—western meadowlark

State Flower—Oregon grape

Postal Abbreviation—OR

Fun Facts:
- Oregon leads the nation in growing a variety of berries and peppermint, and is one of the world's largest suppliers of salmon.
- Oregon has the only nickel smelter in the nation.

OR ★ Salem

Bookmark # 14-38

★ STATES ★

Pennsylvania

Became the 2nd state on December 12, 1787

Nickname—Keystone State

Motto—Virtue, liberty, and independence

Capital—Harrisburg

State Bird—ruffed grouse

State Flower—mountain laurel

Postal Abbreviation—PA

Fun Facts:
- Pennsylvania leads the nation in specialty steel production.
- Attractions in Pennsylvania include Gettysburg, Independence Hall, the Pennsylvania Dutch area, and Valley Forge.

PA ★ Harrisburg

Bookmark # 14-39

★ STATES ★

Rhode Island

Became the 13th state on May 29, 1790

Nickname—Ocean State

Motto—Hope

Capital—Providence

State Bird—Rhode Island red (chicken)

State Flower—violet

Postal Abbreviation—RI

Fun Facts:
- Roger Williams founded Providence after Puritans banished him from Massachusetts.
- The government of Rhode Island refused to take an active part in the War of 1812.
- Rhode Island's name may come from Greece's Island of Rhodes.

RI ★ Providence

Bookmark # 14-40

★ STATES ★

South Carolina

Became the 8th state on May 23, 1788

Nickname—Palmetto State

Mottoes—Prepared in mind and resources; While I breathe, I hope

Capital—Columbia

State Bird—Carolina wren

State Flower—Carolina jessamine

Postal Abbreviation—SC

Fun Facts:
- South Carolina was the first of seven states to secede from the Union before the Civil War began.

SC ★ Columbia

Bookmark # 14-41

SECTION IV: GEOGRAPHY AND FAMOUS PLACES

★ ★ STATES ★ ★

South Dakota

Became the 40th state on November 2, 1889

Nicknames—Coyote State and Mount Rushmore State

Motto—Under God the people rule

Capital—Pierre

State Bird—red-necked pheasant

State Flower—American pasqueflower

Postal Abbreviation—SD

Fun Facts:
- The "Dakota" in South Dakota is from a Sioux word meaning "friends."

Bookmark # 14-42

★ ★ STATES ★ ★

Tennessee

Became the 16th state on June 1, 1796

Nickname—Volunteer State

Motto—Agriculture and Commerce

Capital—Nashville

State Bird—mockingbird

State Flower—iris

Postal Abbreviation—TN

Fun Facts:
- Tennessee is first in the United States in the production of ball clay, marble, pyrite, and zinc.
- Attractions in Tennessee include Graceland, The Grand Ole Opry, and Smoky Mountains National Park.

Bookmark # 14-43

★ ★ STATES ★ ★

Texas

Became the 28th state on December 29, 1845

Nickname—Lone Star State

Motto—Friendship

Capital—Austin

State Bird—mockingbird

State Flower—bluebonnet

Postal Abbreviation—TX

Fun Facts:
- Texas leads the nation in production of oil, cattle, sheep, and cotton.
- Texas shares much of its border with Mexico. Nearly one-third of the population of Texas is Hispanic.

Bookmark # 14-44

★ ★ STATES ★ ★

Utah

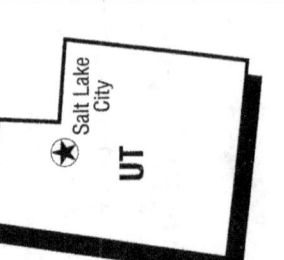

Became the 44th state on January 4, 1896

Nickname—Beehive State

Motto—Industry

Capital—Salt Lake City

State Bird—seagull

State Flower—sego lily

Postal Abbreviation—UT

Fun Facts:
- Utah's name comes from a Ute word meaning "people of the mountains."
- Mormons who fled religious persecution arrived in Utah in 1847.

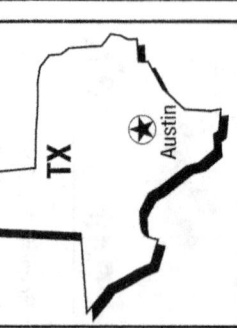

Bookmark # 14-45

★ ★ STATES ★ ★

Vermont

Became the 14th state on March 4, 1791

Nickname—Green Mountain State

Motto—Vermont, Freedom and Unity

Capital—Montpelier

State Bird—hermit thrush

State Flower—red clover

Postal Abbreviation—VT

Fun Facts:
- Vermont is known for its maple syrup, monument granite, and marble.

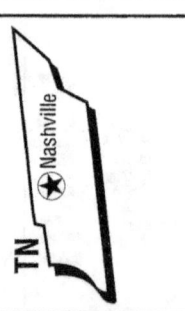

Bookmark # 14-46

★ STATES ★

Virginia

Became the 10th state on June 25, 1788

Nicknames—Mother of the Presidents and Old Dominion

Motto—Thus always to tyrants

Capital—Richmond

State Bird—cardinal

State Flower—dogwood

Postal Abbreviation—VA

Fun Facts:
- Both the American Revolution and the Civil War ended with the signing of surrenders in Virginia.
- Richmond was the capital of the Confederacy.
- Virginia was home to eight U.S. presidents.

VA — Richmond

Bookmark # 14-47

★ STATES ★

Washington

Became the 42nd state on November 11, 1899

Nickname—Evergreen State

Motto—Al-Ki, Native American word meaning "by and by"

Capital—Olympia

State Bird—willow goldfinch

State Flower—coast rhododendron

Postal Abbreviation—WA

Fun Facts:
- Washington is known for its supply of apples, sweet cherries, and other fruits and vegetables.

WA — Olympia

Bookmark # 14-48

★ STATES ★

West Virginia

Became the 35th state on June 20, 1863

Nickname—Mountain State

Motto—Mountaineers are always free

Capital—Charleston

State Bird—cardinal

State Flower—rhododendron

Postal Abbreviation—WV

Fun Facts:
- West Virginia was a part of Virginia until Virginia seceded from the Union.

WV — Charleston

Bookmark # 14-49

★ STATES ★

Wisconsin

Became the 30th state on May 29, 1848

Nickname—Badger State

Motto—Forward

Capital—Madison

State Bird—robin

State Flower—wood violet

Postal Abbreviation—WI

Fun Facts:
- Wisconsin produces more than one-fourth of the nation's cheese.
- About 15% of Wisconsin consists of public parks and forests.
- Attractions in Wisconsin include the Circus World Museum, the House on the Rock, and the Wisconsin Dells.

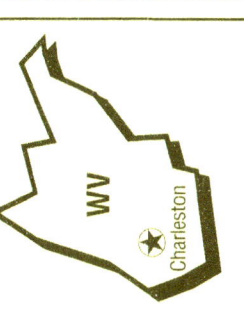
WI — Madison

Bookmark # 14-50

★ STATES ★

Wyoming

Became the 44th state on July 10, 1890

Nickname—Equality State

Motto—Equal rights

Capital—Cheyenne

State Bird—Meadowlark

State Flower—Indian paintbrush

Postal Abbreviation—WY

Fun Facts:
- Nellie Tayloe Ross of Wyoming became the first woman governor in the nation in 1925.
- Wyoming has the world's largest deposits of sodium carbonate (used to soften water and make soap).

WY — Cheyenne

Bookmark # 14-51

SECTION IV: GEOGRAPHY AND FAMOUS PLACES

Bookmark # 15-1

MISCELLANEOUS — EQUATOR — GEOGRAPHY

- The equator is an imaginary line circling Earth's middle. The equator divides the planet into northern and southern hemispheres.
- The equator is 24,903 miles around, which is 42 miles more than the circumference of Earth measuring around the North and South Poles.
- More than two-thirds of Earth's land area lies north of the equator.

LOOKS JUST LIKE THE MAP! EQUATOR

Bookmark # 15-2

MISCELLANEOUS — MAPS — GEOGRAPHY

- Maps are among the first written records people made.
- Maps can show roads or other physical features, political or social differences, or other characteristics.
- Early maps had instructions, such as "one mile past the fallen pine tree."
- The Gulf Oil Company distributed the first map similar to the road maps of today in 1914. They provided the maps without charge.

ONE MILE PAST THE FALLEN PINE TREE?

Bookmark # 15-3

MISCELLANEOUS — THE LARGEST — GEOGRAPHY

OCEANS:
- Pacific
- Atlantic
- Indian
- Arctic

RIVERS:
- Nile in Africa
- Amazon in South America
- Chan Jiang in China
- Yenesey in Russia
- Mississippi in North America

DESERTS:
- Sahara in North Africa—3,500,000 sq. mi.
- Gobi (mostly) in Mongolia—500,000 sq. mi.
- Australian—420,000 sq. mi. (sum of three Australian deserts)
- Kalahari in South Africa—225,000 sq. mi.
- Arabian in Egypt—70,000 sq. mi.

Bookmark # 15-4

MISCELLANEOUS — MORE OF THE LARGEST — GEOGRAPHY

MOUNTAINS:
- Everest in the Himalayas of Nepal—29,028 ft.
- K2 (Godwin Austen) in the Karakoramin of China/Pakistan/India—28,250 ft.
- Kanchenjunga in the Himalayas of Nepal—28,208 ft.
- Makalu in the Himalayas of Nepal—27,824 ft.
- Dhalagiri in the Himalayas of Nepal—26,810 ft.

ISLANDS:
- Greenland in the North Atlantic—840,004 sq. mi.
- New Guinea in the Southwest Pacific—316,856 sq. mi.
- Borneo in the Southwest Pacific—288,243 sq. mi.
- Madagascar in the Indian Ocean—226,658 sq. mi.
- Baffin Island in the Canadian Arctic—183,810 sq. mi.

Bookmark # 16-1

FAMOUS PLACES AND ATTRACTIONS

7 Wonders of the Ancient World

- Pyramids at Giza, Egypt
- Hanging Gardens of Babylon
- Temple of Artemis at Ephesus (now a part of Turkey)
- Statue of Zeus in Olympia, Greece
- Mausoleum of Halicarnassus (now a part of Turkey)
- Colossus of Rhodes in Greece
- Lighthouse of Alexandria, Egypt

FAMOUS PLACES AND ATTRACTIONS

Other Marvels of the World

- Colosseum in Rome, Italy
- Leaning Tower of Piza in Italy
- Parthenon in Athens, Greece
- Santa Sophia (church) in Istanbul, Turkey
- Stonehenge in Salisbury Plain, England
- Taj Mahal in Agra, India

Bookmark # 16-2

FAMOUS PLACES AND ATTRACTIONS

The Alamo

- The Alamo was originally a Spanish mission called San Antonio de Valero.
- While Texans tried to gain their independence from Mexico, many took refuge at the mission. For 13 days in early 1836, about 2,000 Mexicans attacked the soldiers at the Alamo.
- At the end of the battle on March 6, 1836, all 189 men who defended the Alamo against the Mexicans had lost their lives.
- Legend is that the Texans yelled "Remember the Alamo" as they went into the Battle of San Jacinto on April 21, 1836.

Bookmark # 16-3

FAMOUS PLACES AND ATTRACTIONS

Alcatraz

- Alcatraz Prison, built on a 22-acre island in San Francisco Bay in 1933 and closed in 1963, was considered the most escape-proof prison of its time.
- No proof exists of anyone succeeding in escaping Alcatraz. Three men escaped the island in 1962, but are believed to have drowned.
- Alcatraz had 336 regular cells. Each 5 ft. x 3 ft. cell contained a narrow bed, a small table, a toilet, and a sink. An additional 42 cells were reserved for solitary confinement.

Bookmark # 16-4

FAMOUS PLACES AND ATTRACTIONS

Blarney Stone

- The Blarney Stone is located below the battlements on the southern wall of Blarney Castle in County Cork, Ireland.
- According to legend, anyone who lies on his or her back and is lowered to the Blarney Stone to be able to kiss it will be able to influence others.
- The legend is so well known, that *blarney* is a term meaning "flattery."

Bookmark # 16-5

FAMOUS PLACES AND ATTRACTIONS

Eiffel Tower

- Gustave Eiffel, who designed the Eiffel Tower, also designed the right arm of the Statue of Liberty as well as the steel structure that holds "Miss Liberty" together.
- More people of the world recognize a picture of the Eiffel Tower than any other structure.
- Painting the Eiffel Tower takes 6,000 gallons of paint, 60 painters, and four months to complete.

Bookmark # 16-6

SECTION IV: GEOGRAPHY AND FAMOUS PLACES

FAMOUS PLACES AND ATTRACTIONS

Liberty Bell

- Thomas Lister made a bell that had to be melted down and recast twice before it could be rung successfully.
- On July 8, 1776, the bell rang to call people to the first public reading of the Declaration of Independence.
- The bell, which was not called the Liberty Bell until 1839, cracked again in 1846 when it was rung for George Washington's birthday in February. Some sources say it cracked when it was rung for the funeral of Chief Justice John Marshall in July.
- The Liberty Bell is two feet, three inches high and twelve feet around the base. The bell weighs 2,080 pounds.

Bookmark # 16-7

FAMOUS PLACES AND ATTRACTIONS

Mississippi River

- The Mississippi River starts as a small stream in Lake Itasca, Minnesota, and runs 2,348 miles south to the Gulf of Mexico.
- The Mississippi River and its tributaries pass through 31 states and cover about 15,000 miles, earning the river the nickname "The Father of Waters."
- Much of Mark Twain's book *Adventures of Huckleberry Finn* takes place on the Mississippi River.

Bookmark # 16-8

FAMOUS PLACES AND ATTRACTIONS

Mount Rushmore

- Gutzon Borglum designed a monument to U.S. presidents. Drilling on a mountainside near Rapid City, South Dakota, began in August 1927. President Calvin Coolidge took part in the dedication ceremony.
- In 1941, World War II brought a halt to the construction. Mount Rushmore is still not complete according to Borglum's original design.
- The four presidents featured on Mount Rushmore are Thomas Jefferson, Abraham Lincoln, Theodore Roosevelt, and George Washington.

Bookmark # 16-9

FAMOUS PLACES AND ATTRACTIONS

Panama Canal

- Hernando Cortés was the first to propose a water route between the Gulf of Mexico and the Pacific. This route required the building of a canal.
- A company from France started the project, but the company ran out of money. The United States took formal possession of the project in 1904. Work on the canal began two years later.

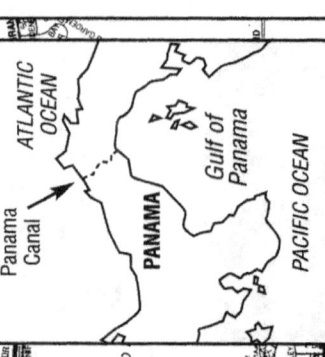

Bookmark # 16-10

FAMOUS PLACES AND ATTRACTIONS

Plymouth Rock

- The *Mayflower* arrived at Plymouth, Massachusetts, on December 22, 1620. The Pilgrims likely didn't step off the ship onto Plymouth Rock, but at the mouth of a nearby brook.
- In 1774, the rock was moved to the Meeting House Square. In 1834, after many people chipped off pieces of the rock as souvenirs, the rock was moved to the front of Pilgrim Hall for better protection.
- Plymouth Rock fell and broke in two during both moves. The halves were cemented together in 1880.

Bookmark # 16-11

FAMOUS PLACES AND ATTRACTIONS

Pyramids

- Egyptians built the pyramids nearly 5,000 years ago as tombs for pharaohs. The square base and four sloping triangular sides were built of stone to protect the mummy and treasures from thieves.
- The Great Pyramid contained about two million stone blocks. All construction was done using muscle power, ropes, and pulleys.
- The first pyramid was built for the Pharaoh Zoser at Sakkara. The pyramid has six steps on the top of it in the belief the Zoser's sprit could climb the steps to the stars.

Bookmark # 16-12

FAMOUS PLACES AND ATTRACTIONS

The Smithsonian Institution

- A British scientist named James Smithson donated the money for a museum. President James Polk signed the act establishing the Smithsonian Institution in 1846.
- The Smithsonian consists of 16 museums and art galleries, as well as the National Zoo. All of the divisions are located in Washington, DC, except for two located in New York City.
- The Smithsonian contains more than 140 million items, of which about two million are on display at any given time.

Bookmark # 16-13

FAMOUS PLACES AND ATTRACTIONS

Statue of Liberty

- The people of France raised $250,000 for a gift of a statue to the people of the United States. The statue was to celebrate the 100th anniversary of the Declaration of Independence.
- The Statue of Liberty, designed by Frederic Auguste Bartholdi, arrived in New York on June 17, 1885.
- The statue was set up on Bedloe's Island, now called Liberty Island.
- The Statue of Liberty is 305 feet tall from the bottom of the base to the top of the torch. The weight of the copper in the statue weighs 31 tons, the steel weighs 125 tons, and the concrete foundation weighs about 27,000 tons.

Bookmark # 16-14

FAMOUS PLACES AND ATTRACTIONS

Stonehenge

- Stonehenge is a circle of about 70 stones, each weighing between 30 and 50 tons, located in Southern England.
- The circle of stones, built about 4,000 years ago, may have been built in its specific pattern for astronomical or religious reasons.

Bookmark # 16-15

FAMOUS PLACES AND ATTRACTIONS

Vietnam Veterans Memorial

- The Vietnam Veterans Memorial in Washington, DC, consists of a flag, a bronze statue of soldiers, and a wall containing the names of more than 58,000 people who were killed or are still missing as a result of the Vietnam War.
- A 21-year-old architectural student named Maya Lin submitted the winning design for the memorial.
- The groundbreaking for the memorial took place on March 26, 1982. The dedication ceremony took place on November 13, 1982.

Bookmark # 16-16

SECTION IV: GEOGRAPHY AND FAMOUS PLACES | 55

FAMOUS PLACES AND ATTRACTIONS

Yellowstone National Park

- The warm lakes and geysers fascinated original explorers to the area that became Yellowstone National Park. One legend is of a lake with water so warm that any fish caught from it was already cooked.
- Ulysses S. Grant signed an act to preserve the area, located mostly in Wyoming, as a "public park or pleasuring ground" in 1872. Yellowstone became the world's first national park to be established.
- Old Faithful, a geyser in Yellowstone, shoots warm, smelly water into the air about every 70 minutes.

Bookmark # 16-19

FAMOUS PLACES AND ATTRACTIONS

The White House

- George Washington selected the location for The White House. Building began on October 13, 1792, but eight years passed before enough had been completed for John and Abigail Adams to move in.
- At first The White House was called "The President's Palace" or "The President's House." It became known as The White House when it was rebuilt after British troops set fire to the building in 1814.
- The White House has 132 rooms, including 11 bedrooms and 33 bathrooms.

Bookmark # 16-18

FAMOUS PLACES AND ATTRACTIONS

Washington Monument

- The Washington Monument is about 555 feet high. The base is just over 55 feet wide, and the top is about 34 feet wide.
- The Washington Monument has 897 steps.
- To protect the Washington Monument from lightning, the building is equipped with 144 platinum-tipped lightning rods.

Bookmark # 16-17

Section V

Physical and Earth Sciences

ASTRONOMY — Mercury
- Mercury is the smallest planet and the planet closest to the Sun.
- A day on Mercury is about 58 Earth days long. It has 88 Earth days in its year.
- Temperatures on Mercury reach 800 degrees Fahrenheit.
- Mercury's surface looks similar to that of Earth's moon, but Mercury doesn't have a moon of its own.

Bookmark # 17-3

ASTRONOMY — Mars
- Mars, "the Red Planet," is 34,090,000 miles away from Earth.
- An Earth day on Mars is about 24 hours and 37 minutes long. Mars has 687 Earth days in a year.
- Temperatures on Mars reach up to 60 degrees Fahrenheit and down to 220 degrees below zero in the same day.
- The largest mountain in the solar system is on Mars. The volcano, likely extinct, is 17 miles high and 370 miles across the base.
- Someone who weighs 100 pounds on Earth would weigh only 38 pounds on Mars.

Bookmark # 17-2

ASTRONOMY — Jupiter
- Jupiter is the largest of the planets. The other eight planets could all fit inside Jupiter at the same time.
- An Earth day on Jupiter is just under 10 hours long, and a year is about 12 Earth years long.
- The red spot on Jupiter is about 25,800 miles wide. Astronomers think the red spot is the center of a violent hurricane.
- Jupiter has at least 16 moons. Four of the moons can be seen with strong binoculars or a small telescope.
- One pound on Jupiter is 2.53 Earth pounds.

Bookmark # 17-1

Neptune

- Astronomers didn't discover Neptune until 1846. They noticed some unexplained movements of Uranus showing the gravitational pull of another planet affecting it. Two astronomers discovered Neptune about the same time.
- A day on Neptune is about 16 Earth hours long. Neptune takes about 165 Earth years to orbit the sun.
- Winds on Neptune blow at a rate of up to 1,500 miles per hour.
- The "great dark spot" on Neptune, similar to Jupiter's great red spot, was a long-lasting storm. In 1994, the Hubble Space Telescope found that the Great Dark Spot had vanished.

Bookmark # 17-4

Pluto

- Pluto takes about 249 Earth years to revolve around the sun.
- Pluto is the only planet that has not been visited by a spacecraft.
- Every 248 years Neptune and Pluto swap places. For about 20 years, Pluto becomes the eighth planet and Neptune the ninth.
- There have been scientific debates about whether Pluto is really a planet.

Bookmark # 17-5

Saturn

- Saturn is the farthest planet that can be seen from Earth without a telescope.
- A year on Saturn is 29 Earth years long.
- Saturn's rings make it distinctive from the other planets. The rings are narrow bands of debris made up of mostly rocks and ice. The rings may be no more than a few hundred feet thick. The rings reflect light, which makes them look larger.

Bookmark # 17-6

Uranus

- The planet of Uranus was discovered by accident in 1781.
- Uranus looks blue-green due to methane and high altitude photochemical smog.
- Nine narrow rings similar to those on Saturn surround Uranus.
- A day on Uranus is 17 Earth hours long.
- Uranus rotates on its side instead of on an axis the way the other planets do.
- Uranus doesn't follow a predicted orbit because Neptune pulls it.
- Little was known about Uranus until *Voyager 2* flew close to the planet in 1986.

Bookmark # 17-7

Venus

- The closest planet to Earth is Venus, which is about 26 million miles away at the closest point in its orbit.
- Venus takes longer to spin on its axis than it takes to orbit the sun. That means that a day on Venus is longer than a year.
- The temperature on Venus is over 870 degrees Fahrenheit.
- Venus passes between Earth and the Sun every 584 days.
- High-speed winds on Venus are almost always blowing clouds made of droplets of sulfuric acid.

Bookmark # 17-8

The Sun

- The Sun is the star located closest to Earth.
- The core temperature of the Sun is about 15.6 million degrees Centigrade or 28.1 million degrees Fahrenheit. The dark regions, called sunspots, are about 3,230 degrees Centigrade cooler than their surroundings.
- The density of the Sun is about 1 1/4 times that of water, or 1/4 the average density of Earth.
- More than one million Earths would fit inside the Sun. The Sun's radius is about 432,169 miles or 109.3 times Earth's radius, giving the Sun 1,306,000 times the volume of Earth. The Sun's mass is 333,400 times as great as that of Earth.
- The blue part of the Sun's light scatters better than the red part, making Earth's daytime sky blue.

Bookmark # 17-9

Earth's Moon

- The Moon's diameter is 2,160 miles, making it about 1/4 the size of Earth, but its mass is less than 1/80 that of Earth.
- Temperatures on the sunny side of the Moon are near the boiling point (260 degrees Fahrenheit) while temperatures on the dark side are very cold (minus 280 degrees Fahrenheit).
- Craters on the Moon range from 1/4 mile across to 183 miles across. The craters were made from meteors or possibly volcanoes.

Bookmark # 17-10

Stars

- The total number of stars in Earth's galaxy is in the billions.
- The light of stars is made by nuclear reactions similar to that of a bomb when hydrogen is changed into helium.
- The Sun is Earth's nearest star at about 93 million miles away. The next nearest visible star is Alpha Centauri, which is more than 4 light years away.

Bookmark # 17-11

EARTH

- weight—6,600,000,000,000,000,000,000 tons (6 septillion, 587 quintillion tons)
- surface area—about 196,950,000 square miles
- circumference—24,902 miles around the equator and 24,860 miles around the poles
- distance to the center of Earth (radius)—about 3,950 miles
- diameter at Equator—7,926.42 miles
- distance from the Sun—92,900,000 miles
- distance from the Moon—238,854 miles
- orbit around the Sun—583,400,000 miles
- rotation speed—up to 1,030 miles per hour at the equator (0.289 miles per second)
- speed in orbit—about 66,600 miles per hour (18.5 miles per second)

Bookmark # 18-1

ATMOSPHERE

Earth's atmosphere becomes thinner the higher the altitude. The four main zones:

- The troposphere rises 10-11 miles above Earth and helps create the weather. It is about 10 miles at the Equator and about 5 miles at the Poles.
- The stratosphere begins 8-12 miles above Earth and extends up to 30 miles. From 30 miles to 50 miles, it is known as the mesosphere and absorbs harmful radiation.
- The ionosphere (also called thermosphere) is located 50-400 miles above Earth and reflects radio waves.
- The exosphere is located more than 400 miles above Earth and merges with interplanetary space.

Bookmark # 18-2

EARTH

CAVES

- Caves are caused by moving water, either underground streams or ocean waves.
- The deepest caves in the world are in France, where many caves are more than 3,000 feet deep.
- The longest known cave in the world is Mammoth Cave in Kentucky at 150 miles long. It has 348 miles of charted passageways.
- Rhode Island is the only state that doesn't have at least one of the 12,000 known caves in the United States.

Bookmark # 18-3

EARTH

GLACIERS

- Glaciers are formed when summers aren't warm enough to completely melt the winter's snow. More and more ice builds up until a glacier is formed.
- Most of the world's glaciers are in Antarctica, where sheets of ice are thousands of yards thick.
- Glaciers are sometimes called "rivers of ice" because they move slowly.
- Glaciers normally move very slowly (about three feet a day), but the Black Rapids Glacier in Alaska moved more than 100 feet per day.

HURRY IT UP, WILL YA?

Bookmark # 18-4

EARTH

ICEBERGS

- Icebergs are huge chunks of ice that break off from glaciers.
- The largest iceberg ever seen was over 208 miles long and 60 miles wide. It was sighted in November 1956, in the Ross Sea of Antarctica.
- Icebergs from Antarctica are usually larger than those from the Arctic.
- An iceberg caused the sinking of the ship *Titanic*.

Bookmark # 18-5

EARTH

OCEANS

- Over 70% of Earth's surface is covered in water.
- The water in the oceans is salty.
- The average depth of the oceans is 16,000 feet below sea level. If the water were spread evenly over Earth, about 8 feet of water would cover all surfaces.
- The Pacific Ocean alone covers more area (166 million sq. mi.) than all the dry land on Earth. The Pacific Ocean is three times larger than Asia, the largest continent. The greatest width is 11,000 miles, from Panama to the Malay Peninsula.

WATER, WATER EVERYWHERE!

Bookmark # 18-6

EARTH

RAIN FORESTS

- Rain forests have rich soil, and are very warm and moist. These conditions allow plants to grow well.
- Although rain forests make up only about 5% of Earth's surface, they are home to 65% of all kinds of plants and animals.
- As rain forests are destroyed by pollution or harvesting, animals are losing their habitats. Several species are now endangered or extinct.
- Losing the rain forests can affect the weather around the world and change the air people breathe.

Bookmark # 18-7

---

60 | BOOKMARKS ACROSS THE CURRICULUM

EARTH

ROCKS

Rocks come in three general types:

- **sedimentary**—formed when grains of soil are pressed together; the most common type of rock
- **igneous**—formed by the cooling of molten magma from Earth's interior; most igneous rocks are formed after the eruption of volcanoes, but can be formed inside Earth
- **metamorphic**—formed by changes in temperature, pressure, or chemical activity; this type of rock is the most rare

Bookmark # 18-8

WEATHER NATURAL PHENOMENA

Avalanches

- An avalanche is a sudden fall of snow or ice down the side of a mountain.
- An avalanche is caused when so much snow falls that the layers of snow get too heavy and suddenly give way. Earthquakes, sudden loud noises, and melting snow can start an avalanche.
- Avalanches can carry rocks, uprooted trees, and anything else in their paths, making them even more dangerous.

Bookmark # 19-1

WEATHER NATURAL PHENOMENA

Clouds

Clouds are simply fog floating in the sky and are categorized by three main types:

- **cumulus**—heaped up in thick piles above a flat base; these are the clouds in which various shapes can be seen with some imagination
- **cirrus**—feathery clouds high in the sky
- **stratus**—spread out in layers of dark or gray streaks close to Earth's surface; these clouds usually mean storms or rain

These main types of clouds can combine to form other types.

Bookmark # 19-2

WEATHER NATURAL PHENOMENA

Earthquakes

An earthquake happens when energy stored in large layers of rocks is released, causing the rocks to move, which sets up vibrations. The strength of an earthquake is measured by the Richter magnitude scale using various levels.

- A level 2 earthquake likely would be noticed only by machines.
- People would be aware of a level 5 earthquake, but the quake likely would do little damage.
- Rocks likely couldn't store more energy than would be released in a level 9 earthquake.

Bookmark # 19-3

WEATHER NATURAL PHENOMENA

San Francisco Earthquake

San Francisco, California, is located on the San Andreas Fault. At 5:13 A.M. on April 18, 1906, a major earthquake hit San Francisco. The earthquake caused much damage, but the resulting fire created the most damage. The fire burned out of control for three days until rain quenched the fire. About 700 people died, 250,000 people were left homeless, and over 28,000 buildings were destroyed by the earthquake and fire. The earthquake was later estimated to measure 7.9 on the Richter scale.

Bookmark # 19-4

SECTION V: PHYSICAL AND EARTH SCIENCE | 61

WEATHER NATURAL PHENOMENA

Hurricanes

- Hurricanes consist of powerful winds, thunder, lightning, driving rain, and raging seas. For a storm to be classified as a hurricane, winds have to be at least 74 miles per hour. Hurricane winds often reach over 150 miles per hour.
- Hurricanes begin in warm seas and moist winds of the tropics near the equator.
- An entire hurricane can be over 500 miles across, but the average is about 300 miles across.
- The center of the storm, called the "eye," is about 15 miles across and very calm.

Bookmark # 19-5

WEATHER NATURAL PHENOMENA

Lightning

- Lightning is a random discharge of static electricity. Lightning equalizes the electrostatic state within a storm.
- Lightning has two types: strikes that travel from the cloud to the ground and strikes that don't travel to the ground.
- Thunder is the sound made when a shock wave occurs from the heat of lightning—sometimes as hot as 18,000 degrees Fahrenheit.

Bookmark # 19-6

WEATHER NATURAL PHENOMENA

Lightning Safety

- Some rules of lightning safety include
- Don't go outdoors; stay in your home or car (the rubber tires offer protection).
- Don't use the telephone.
- Unplug appliances such as televisions and computers.
- Don't stand near or hold metal objects, such as flag poles and umbrellas.
- If on a boat, get off the water as soon as possible.
- Stay away from the highest object, such as a tree, in an area; make yourself as small an object as possible.

Bookmark # 19-7

WEATHER NATURAL PHENOMENA

Northern Lights

- Northern lights are green, pink, and yellow lights that flash from the horizon and spread upward 60 to 600 miles into the sky. The spectacular show can last a few hours or all night.
- Northern lights are caused when atomic particles from solar flares near sunspots hit thin gases in the upper atmosphere.
- Northern lights appear more frequently the closer an observer gets to the North Pole, although a similar light show can be seen in the Southern Hemisphere.

Bookmark # 19-8

WEATHER NATURAL PHENOMENA

Rain

- The weight of all the water that falls on one acre of land during a one-inch rainfall would weigh 226,000 pounds.
- An island in the Indian Ocean (Cherrapunji) once got more than 6 feet of rain in a single day. It averages 87 feet per year.
- In 1956, part of Maryland received over one inch of rain in one minute.
- Acid rain is caused by chemicals in polluted air. As the rain falls through the air, it dissolves the chemicals and carries them to Earth. These chemicals make precipitation more acidic than usual. Acid rain is harmful to buildings, water, trees and other plants, and all animals, including humans.

Bookmark # 19-9

WEATHER NATURAL PHENOMENA

Rainbows

- Rainbows are formed by refraction of sunlight through falling raindrops.
- According to the Bible, God sent a rainbow as a promise that He would not send another flood to cover Earth.
- So far no one has found the mythical pot of gold said to be at the end of a rainbow.

Bookmark # 19-10

Tornadoes

- Tornadoes, also called twisters or cyclones, are caused when warm, moist air from the south is trapped under colder, heavier air from the north.
- A tornado forms when the swirling winds of a thunderstorm create a vacuum. The winds can reach 300-500 miles an hour.
- The tornado starts out white in color and turns dark as it sucks up debris along its zigzag path. The tornado's tail touching the ground causes the destruction.
- A funnel cloud looks like a tornado, but doesn't touch the ground.

Bookmark # 19-11

Volcanoes

- About 1,511 volcanoes above sea level have been active during the past 10,000 years. Many of them are now inactive.
- The two main types of volcanic eruptions are effusive, where lava flows slowly from the volcano's mouth, and explosive, where material is launched into the air in an eruption column.
- In 1883, the Krakatoa volcano in Indonesia exploded. The sound could be heard 3,100 miles away. About 36,000 people were killed by the volcano, most of them from the 118-foot-high tidal wave caused by the volcano.

Bookmark # 19-12

Mount St. Helens

- Mount St. Helens, a volcano near the border of Oregon and Washington, erupted on May 18, 1980.
- The top 1,200 feet of the mountain were blown to bits.
- The cloud of ash from the eruption was nearly 12 miles high.
- More than 70 square miles of land was destroyed. The flowing mud blocked rivers and streams, destroyed forests and farmland, and killed 57 people.

Bookmark # 19-13

Weather Vanes

- Weather vanes are designed so that the head or front of the shape points into the wind to show the direction from which the wind is blowing.
- Weather vanes can be made of metal, wood, plastic, or other materials.
- The shape of roosters on churches in the ninth century is a reminder of the cock that crowed when St. Peter denied Christ three times.
- Weather vanes come in many shapes besides roosters, including horses and other animals, cars, and arrows.

Bookmark # 19-14

SECTION V: PHYSICAL AND EARTH SCIENCE | 63

PHYSICS

Light

- The spectrum is a band of the seven different light waves that can be seen. All light waves are of different lengths and produce different colors. The colors can be seen when sunlight shines through a prism or some crystals.
- The colors from longest wavelength to shortest wavelength can be remembered by thinking "ROY G BIV" with the letters representing

Red
Orange
Yellow
Green
Blue
Indigo
Violet

Bookmark # 20-5

PHYSICS

Lasers

- "Laser" stands for
Light
Amplification by
Stimulated
Emission of
Radiation.
- Lasers can be extremely powerful or very weak. Powerful laser beams can be used to cut through thick walls. Weak laser beams are often used in pointer lights.
- Lasers are used in manufacturing, in laboratories, as tools for surgery, and in many other industries.

Bookmark # 20-4

PHYSICS

Nuclear Energy

- Nuclear energy, sometimes called atomic energy, is the most powerful source of any chemical or mechanical energy known at this time.
- The Italian physicist Enrico Fermi built the first nuclear reactor in Chicago, Illinois. The reactor first produced energy in December 1942.
- Nuclear energy is one of the cleanest forms of energy, but also one of the most dangerous.
- One pound of nuclear fuel can produce as much energy as 3.25 million pounds of coal.

Bookmark # 20-3

PHYSICS

Energy Sources

- Wind energy comes from moving air.
- Solar energy comes from the Sun.
- Fossil fuels are the remains of ancient plants and animals that died millions of years ago. Fossil fuels include coal, petroleum, and natural gas. The supply of fossil fuels is limited.
- Hydroelectric power comes from rushing water.
- Nuclear power is made by splitting uranium atoms into smaller atoms.
- Biomass energy comes from wood, animal wastes, and garbage.

Bookmark # 20-2

PHYSICS

Echo

- An echo is a repetition of sound caused by a reflection of sound waves. Echoes usually occur in large empty areas, such as a valley between mountains or an empty stadium.
- A cave in Killarney, Ireland, named The Eagle's Nest, will echo a single sound more than 100 times.
- Many musicians use an echo effect for the quality it gives their music.

Bookmark # 20-1

---

64 | BOOKMARKS ACROSS THE CURRICULUM

PHYSICS

Soap Bubbles

- Bubbles are in an elliptical shape (similar to that of an egg) when they're being blown, but are round when the bubble breaks free. Scientists often use that example to explain why the planets are roughly round.
- The thinnest soap bubbles are 1/2,500,000 inch thick.

PHYSICS

Changing States of Matter

- Freezing happens when a liquid is turned into a solid. The liquid needs to become so cold that the molecules move closer together and stop moving.
- Melting happens when a solid is turned into a liquid. The solid needs to be heated enough so that the molecules move apart and begin moving around.
- Evaporation happens when a liquid changes to a gas. The molecules move more rapidly and farther apart.
- Condensation happens when warm, moist air meets a cool surface and droplets of water form.

PHYSICS

States of Matter

- **solid**—the molecules are packed together tightly; they vibrate but can't change position; the object cannot change shape easily
- **liquid**—the molecules are connected loosely and are able to move around; liquids take the shape of their container
- **gas**—the molecules are not connected to one another and move randomly; gases can be invisible and are lighter than solids and liquids
- **plasma**—the molecules move extremely fast because they are heated to very high temperatures; the Sun is an example of matter in the plasma state

---

PHYSICS

Magnetism

- Magnetism is a force of matter attracting or repelling other matter.
- Every magnet has two poles (north and south). Two north or south poles force each other away. One north pole and one south pole attract.
- Most magnets are made of metal containing steel, iron, cobalt, or nickel. Magnets can be made into almost any shape.
- The needle on a compass is a magnet that points to the North Pole.

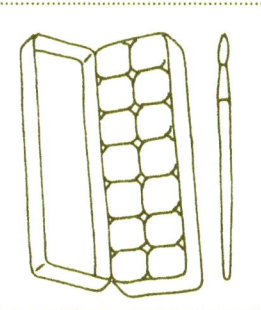
HEY! THE NEEDLE'S FROZEN!

PHYSICS

Colors

Red, green, and blue are the primary colors of light. They can be mixed in different amounts to produce any color of light. Mixing all three colors of light produces white. The three primary pigments are magenta, cyan, and yellow. They can be mixed to produce other pigment colors. Mixing all three primary pigments results in black. Pigments are colored materials that absorb some colors and reflect others. Pigments are used to make paints, for example.

SECTION V: PHYSICAL AND EARTH SCIENCE | 65

Section VI

Life Sciences

PLANTS

Spreading Seeds

Seeds must be spread to ensure growth. Some ways seeds are spread include

- air currents—the wind carries light-weight seeds away from the flower
- animals and people—seeds are spread when they stick to fur or clothing
- droppings—birds or animals eat the seeds, which are spread through their droppings
- exploding seed pods—some seed pods burst and shoot the seeds outward
- water—moving water, such as a stream, can carry seeds several miles

Bookmark # 21-3

PLANTS

Seeds

- Some seeds, such as carrot seeds, are so tiny that they can barely be seen. Other seeds, such as coconuts, are very large.
- Some seeds, such as apple seeds, are inside the fruit of a plant. Other seeds, such as those on a strawberry, are on the outside of the fruit.
- Sometimes people eat the seeds, such as corn, and other times spit out the seeds, such as watermelon.

Bookmark # 21-2

PLANTS

Parts of Some Plants

- anther—produces pollen
- carpels—female parts of the flower
- leaves—collect the sun's energy to create food
- roots—anchor the plant, and pull water and minerals from the soil
- seeds—used for reproduction
- stamen—the male parts of the flower
- stem—provides the main structure of the plant
- stigma—receives the pollen during pollination
- tepals—protect the male and female parts of a flower

Bookmark # 21-1

SECTION VI: LIFE SCIENCES | 67

THE HUMAN BODY

Parts of the Blood

- Plasma is a yellow fluid that carries most of the chemical nutrients.
- Red blood cells are composed of protein and an iron compound called hemoglobin, which transports oxygen. They give the blood its red color.
- White blood cells fight off infection.
- Platelets help blood clot. They are fragments of a type of cell in the bone marrow.
- Substances on the surface of red blood cells determine the blood type. The four blood types are A, B, AB, and O. A type AB person can receive blood of any type. A type O person can give blood to a person of any blood type.

Bookmark # 22-1

PLANTS

Leaves

Deciduous trees are those that lose their leaves in the autumn and grow new leaves in the spring. The leaves seem to change color before they drop off the trees, but in reality they don't change color at all. The leaf's chlorophyll, which helps plants make oxygen, disappears when the leaf dies. The other colors were there all along, but the green-colored chlorophyll hid them.

Bookmark # 21-7

PLANTS

Carnivorous Plants

Carnivorous plants are plants that eat insects or other meat. Two kinds of carnivorous plants:

- The pitcher plant, which has leaves shaped like vases or pitchers, is found mainly in tropical Asia. Small hairs on the plant catch insects when they enter the plant to drink its juice.
- The Venus flytrap has leaves fringed with small teeth. When an insect lands on a leaf, the leaf closes with the insect inside.

Bookmark # 21-6

PLANTS

Cactus

- More than 1,500 different species of cactus are known.
- A desert cactus can survive a long time without water because it has a good root system to absorb water. A cactus stem can hold enough water to last more than two years.
- The spines on a cactus provide shade for the plant, collect raindrops and dew, and protect the plant from predators.
- The biggest cactus in North America is the saguaro, which can grow to 50 feet high and weigh 12,000-14,000 pounds.

Bookmark # 21-5

PLANTS

Bananas

- Bananas are from the same family as lilies, orchids, and palms.
- The stalk of a banana plant is about 93% water. The fruit is about 75% water.
- Bananas grow upward on their stalks.
- The banana plant is the largest plant on Earth without a woody stem. The stalk can grow up to 30 feet high and is very fragile. Even light winds can destroy a banana stalk.

Bookmark # 21-4

THE HUMAN BODY

The Brain

- The brain controls the body, including motion, thought, memory, and emotion.
- The weight of the brain triples between birth and adulthood. The average weight of an adult male brain is 3 pounds and an adult female brain about 2.9 pounds. The size of the brain has no relationship to intelligence.
- A larger proportion of the brain function is devoted to thumb movements than to the whole chest and abdomen.
- The brain processes hundreds of millions of impulses each day.

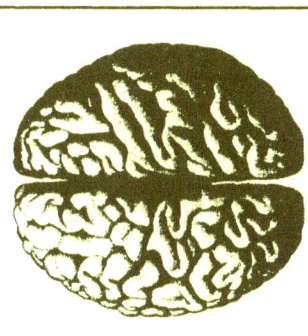

Bookmark # 22-2

The Cells

- Cells generate and process energy, store genetic information, and preserve life functions.
- The human body contains 10 trillion cells, with about 200 different types of cells, such as muscle cells and stomach cells.
- The smallest cell in the body is a red blood cell at 0.000034 inch across.
- About 10,000 average-sized cells can fit on the head of a pin.

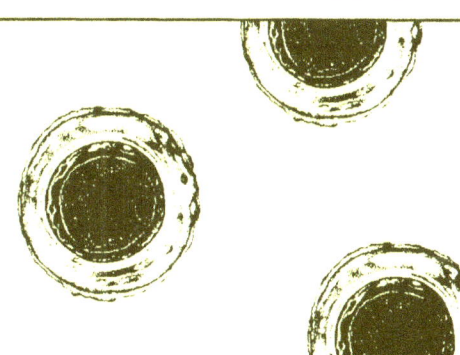

Bookmark # 22-3

The Ear

- Ears aren't used only for hearing, but also to give senses of balance and direction.
- Tiny hairs and wax in the ears help protect them from dust and dirt.
- Three tiny bones in the ear are named for their shapes: hammer, anvil, and stirrup. The stirrup is the smallest bone in the body.

Bookmark # 22-4

The Eye

- The eye doesn't actually "see." The eye carries the images to the brain, which interprets the images and causes us to "see" them.
- The pupil of the eye shrinks in bright light and widens in dim light.
- Rods located in the retina help someone see in dim light. Cones in the eye need bright light to help distinguish colors and details.
- Two-thirds of the information the brain processes comes through the eyes.

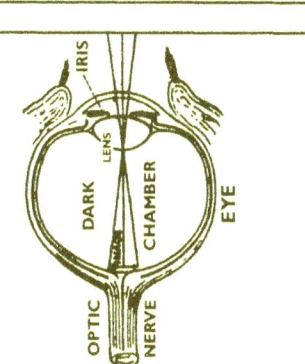

Bookmark # 22-5

Fingerprints

- The chance of someone having the exact fingerprints as someone else is about 64 billion to one.
- Arches, loops, and whorls are the three main patterns used in identifying fingerprints.
- The ancient Assyrians and Chinese used fingerprints to sign legal documents.
- In 1892, a woman in Argentina who murdered someone became the first person to be caught using fingerprints.
- In 1901, Sir Edward Richard Henry started the first collection of people's fingerprints to aid in criminal investigation.

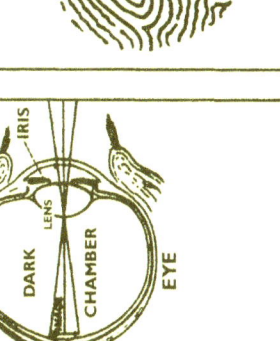

Bookmark # 22-6

SECTION VI: LIFE SCIENCES | 69

THE HUMAN BODY

Hair

- Humans lose 50-100 strands of hair each day.
- Hair grows at a rate of about 3/4 inch per month. The rate of growth slows if the hair is a foot long or more.
- The scalp of blondes has about 150,000 hairs, brunettes 100,000, and redheads 60,000.

Bookmark # 22-7

THE HUMAN BODY

The Heart

- An adult heart beats about 40 million times a year and about 2½ billion times in an average lifetime.
- The heart beats about 70 times per minute in an adult at rest, 100 times a minute in children, and 120 times a minute in babies. An athlete's resting heartbeat is about 40-60 beats per minute.
- The heart pumps more than a gallon of blood through the body every minute.
- The heart pumps blood through 60 miles of blood vessels during the course of a day.

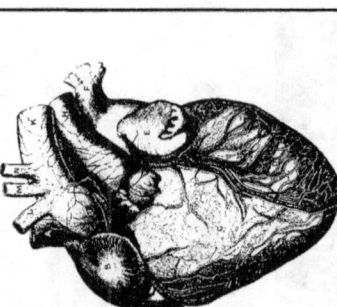

Bookmark # 22-8

THE HUMAN BODY

Respiratory System

- The respiratory system allows oxygen to enter the blood, and takes carbon dioxide and other wastes from the blood.
- The major parts of the respiratory system include the nose, pharynx (throat), larynx (voice box), trachea (windpipe), and lungs.
- The air going out during a sneeze can travel at 100 miles an hour or more.
- Smoking just one cigarette can damage the respiratory system for an hour. Repeated smoking can cause permanent damage.

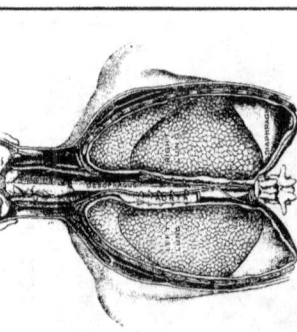

Bookmark # 22-9

THE HUMAN BODY

The Five Senses

- **Sight**—using the eyes to distinguish objects
- **Hearing**—using the ears to listen to sounds
- **Smell**—using the nose to identify scents
- **Taste**—using the tongue to identify sweet, salty, sour, and bitter flavors
- **Touch**—using sensors in the skin to feel a material object

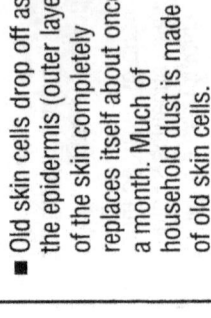

Bookmark # 22-10

THE HUMAN BODY

Skin

- The skin helps keep harmful microorganisms from entering the body, protects the body from the sun, prevents the loss of body fluids, regulates body temperature, excretes some waste products, allows the sense of touch, and more.
- Skin varies from 0.06 inch to 0.16 inch thick.
- The skin on an average adult covers about 22 square feet and weighs about 10 pounds.
- Old skin cells drop off as the epidermis (outer layer) of the skin completely replaces itself about once a month. Much of household dust is made of old skin cells.

Bookmark # 22-11

THE HUMAN BODY

Teeth

An adult human has 32 teeth, 16 in the upper jaw and 16 in the lower jaw, used for eating and making sounds. Types and numbers of teeth are

- **8 incisors**—the sharp front teeth used for biting or cutting
- **8 cuspids**—the pointed "vampire" teeth between the incisors and molars (cuspids are also known as canine teeth because they look like those of a dog); the upper cuspids are also known as eyeteeth
- **4 bicuspids**—flat teeth with points
- **12 molars**—broad back teeth used for chewing food

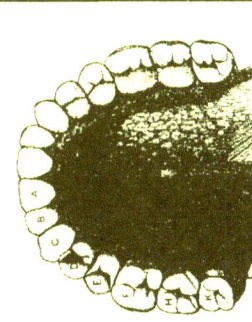

Bookmark # 22-12

THE HUMAN BODY

Tongue

The tongue helps in eating and speaking. Taste buds allow flavors of food to be sensed.

- Bitter flavors are tasted at the back of the tongue.
- Salty flavors are tasted on each side near the front of the tongue.
- Sour flavors are tasted on each side near the back of the tongue.
- Sweet flavors are tasted on the tip of the tongue.

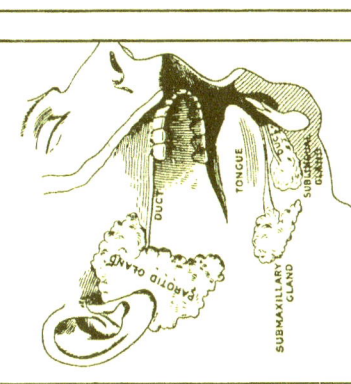

Bookmark # 22-13

AILMENTS AND CONDITIONS

Artificial Limbs

- One of the oldest surgical procedures is cutting off an arm or a leg.
- Artificial limbs were mentioned in Hindu writings dating back 3,500 years.
- Peg legs (a leg without a foot that looked similar to a plain chair leg) were common in the Middle Ages. Legs with a hinge for the knee are a recent development.
- Before World War I, most artificial legs were made of wood. An aluminum alloy was found to be lighter and stronger.
- Now, artificial skin coverings make artificial limbs look and feel more real.

Bookmark # 23-1

AILMENTS AND CONDITIONS

Dentures

- If people lose their teeth to accident or disease, dentures (false teeth) can help them eat and speak more clearly.
- Etruscans of Italy made the first crude dentures about 2,700 years ago.
- Dentures can be made for one tooth or to cover the entire mouth.
- The first full set of dentures similar to those of today were made in France in the 1780s.
- George Washington is said to have had wooden dentures.

Bookmark # 23-2

AILMENTS AND CONDITIONS

Eyeglasses

- The first people known to wear glasses were Mongols in the 13th century.
- The first bifocal glasses were made for Benjamin Franklin, at his request, in 1760.
- Painter Leonardo da Vinci had the idea for contact lenses in the 1500s, but the first contact lenses weren't made until the 1880s.
- Single lenses for one eye are called monocles. Glasses without bows that fit over the ear are called pince-nez, from the French word for "pinch nose." Glasses with a handle are called lorgnettes.

Bookmark # 23-3

SECTION VI: LIFE SCIENCES

Bone Fractures

Rx AILMENTS AND CONDITIONS

- A simple bone fracture is when the bone is broken, but the skin is not cut. Care must be taken that a simple fracture does not become a compound fracture.
- A compound fracture is when the skin near the break is pierced. Care must be taken to prevent infection.
- A splint, a firm object that supports the wounded area, is put on some fractures. Other fractures need to be completely protected and are covered in a cast made of plaster or plastic.

Bookmark # 23-4

Hiccups

Rx AILMENTS AND CONDITIONS

- Hiccups are caused when the diaphragm and muscles between the ribs suddenly contract. The sharp, uncontrollable inhalation of air doesn't reach the lungs because a muscle spasm closes the windpipe. The air is forced upward through the esophagus.
- Hiccups are named for the sound that occurs when the air is released.

Bookmark # 23-5

Left-Handers

Rx AILMENTS AND CONDITIONS

- Some names for people who favor their left hand over their right hand are *sinistrals* (from the Latin for "on the left"), *lefties*, and *southpaws*.
- About one in three people is born left-handed. In the past, parents and teachers trained children to use their right hands instead.
- About 2,500 years ago, the Greek philosopher Plato believed a person would favor the hand his or her mother used to rock the cradle. Scientists have learned that the brain controls which hand someone favors.

Bookmark # 23-6

Snoring

Rx AILMENTS AND CONDITIONS

- Snoring is caused by a vibration of the soft, mobile back part of the roof of the mouth and the arch behind the tonsils.
- In most cases, the snorer's nose is partially blocked, which causes the snorer to breath through the mouth.
- Often, but not always, a snorer is sleeping on his or her back.

Bookmark # 23-7

Twins

Rx AILMENTS AND CONDITIONS

- Fraternal twins are the result of a sperm combining with an egg about the same time another sperm combines with another egg. Except for being the same age, fraternal twins are no more alike than other brothers and sisters.
- Identical twins happen when one egg becomes two babies. Identical twins will look alike.
- Conjoined (Siamese) twins are identical twins that don't completely separate into two babies. Sometimes conjoined twins can be separated by surgery.

Bookmark # 23-8

72 | BOOKMARKS ACROSS THE CURRICULUM

MAMMALS
Armadillo

- Armadillos are part of a group known as *edentates*, meaning "without teeth," even though armadillos do have teeth.
- Armadillos are one of the few mammals without fur. Instead, they have an armor of horny scales.
- Some armadillos roll into a ball when attacked.
- Armadillos build several nests and use them in turn instead of using only one nest at a time.
- The giant armadillo is about three feet long. The fairy armadillo is only about five inches long.

Bookmark # 25-1

DINOSAURS
Why Dinosaurs Disappeared

Many different theories of why the dinosaurs disappeared have been suggested. Some of them are

- radiation from the Sun became stronger and Earth's temperatures grew cooler
- a deadly disease killed them
- food sources were somehow lost
- a giant meteorite hit Earth and the clouds of dust blocked out the Sun long enough so that nothing could grow
- volcanic eruptions produced changes in the climate that didn't allow the dinosaurs to survive

Bookmark # 24-4

DINOSAURS
Some Dinosaurs

- The Allosaurus, meaning "different reptile," reached a length of 39 feet and ate meat.
- The Stegosaurus, meaning "roof lizard," had alternating rows of plates along its back, reached a length of 15 feet, and ate plants.
- The Triceratops, meaning "three-horned face," reached a length of 26 feet and ate plants.
- The Tyrannosaurus, meaning "tyrant lizard," was one of the largest predators to walk Earth, reached a length of 41 feet, and ate meat.

Bookmark # 24-3

DINOSAURS
Dinosaur Fossils

Scientists find the age of dinosaur fossils by

- *chemical dating method*—determines the amount of calcium remaining in a bone
- *radioactive method*—determines the percentage of how much a substance has lost its active qualities
- *stratigraphic method*—compares the location of the fossils in layers of rock with known ages of other fossils

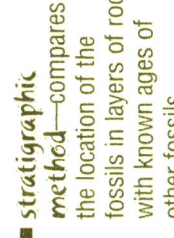

Bookmark # 24-2

DINOSAURS
Dinosaurs

- Sir Richard Owen coined the term *dinosaur*, meaning "terrible lizard," in 1842 after he realized dinosaurs were different from living reptiles.
- Dinosaurs lived on Earth for about 150 million years during the Mesozoic Era.
- Some dinosaurs were about the size of a large rabbit, while others were nearly 100 feet long.
- Even large dinosaurs had small brains.
- Dinosaurs were "bird-hipped" or "lizard-hipped" depending on how their hip bones were placed.

Bookmark # 24-1

SECTION VI: LIFE SCIENCES | 73

MAMMALS
Bat

- Bats are the only mammals that can fly.
- Bats use sound, not vision, to fly around obstacles and to find food. In a process called echolocation, bats make high-pitched squeaking sounds that produce sound waves. These waves bounce off solid objects in front of the bats, helping bats to locate objects.
- To start flying, the bat drops from its perch. Once a bat is flying, it can't stop until it's ready to land on another perch.
- Bats sleep upside down because their legs aren't strong enough to hold them. The vampire bat is the only bat able to walk.

Bookmark # 25-2

MAMMALS
Camel

- Dromedary camels have one hump, while Bactrian camels have two humps.
- The hump or humps on camels are masses of solid fat. The humps nearly disappear when a camel is starved.
- Camels have two rows of eyelashes to protect their eyes from sand. Camels can also close their nostrils to keep out sand.

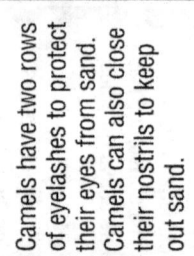

Bookmark # 25-3

MAMMALS
Cat

- Cats walk only on their toes, unlike humans who walk on their heels and toes.
- Cats have about 40 more bones than humans. The extra bones make them more flexible.
- Cats have excellent hearing. The 32 muscles in each ear let the ears swivel to be able to zero in on sounds.
- At night, cats can see about six times better than humans.
- Cats spend about 18 hours a day sleeping. About 30% of a cat's time awake is spent cleaning itself.
- White cats with blue eyes are often deaf.
- Calico cats are almost always female.

Bookmark # 25-4

MAMMALS
Cheetah

- Scientists once thought cheetahs were part dog and part cat.
- A cheetah can reach a speed of 45 miles per hour in two seconds. A cheetah can run up to 70 miles per hour for short distances.
- Cheetahs are the only cats whose claws aren't hidden by sheaths. Cheetahs need their claws to grip the ground when running, which helps their speed.

Bookmark # 25-5

MAMMALS
Chimpanzee

- Chimpanzees are the smallest of the great apes and are closely related to humans.
- The facial expressions on chimps are clues to their emotions, although they don't shed tears when they're sad.
- Chimpanzee babies stay with their mother up to 10 years and even visit their mother after they leave the group.
- Chimps are one of the few animals that use tools. One example is putting a stick in a termite mound and eating the insects as they crawl up the stick.

Bookmark # 25-6

74 | BOOKMARKS ACROSS THE CURRICULUM

MAMMALS
Dolphin

- At least 32 species of dolphins are known.
- Dolphins can live deep in the ocean or in large rivers.
- Dolphins can live 40 years or longer.
- Thousands of dolphins are killed each year when they're caught in tuna nets.
- Dolphins can hear well, but have no sense of smell and little sense of taste. They use sound echoes to find food.
- Dolphins don't have vocal cords, but can make clicking noises and whistles. Some dolphins have been known to communicate with humans.

Bookmark # 25-11

MAMMALS
Dogs in Police Work

Dogs who work on the police force must be tested thoroughly. Some of the things for which dogs must pass strict standards are

- alertness and response time
- interest and enthusiasm
- obedience
- agility and tracking ability
- scent detection

JUST THE FACTS, MA'AM...

Bookmark # 25-10

MAMMALS
Dog

- Dogs sweat through the pads of their feet and pant to cool themselves.
- Dogs' noseprints are as different from one another as human fingerprints are. A dog's noseprint is more accurate than a paw print.
- Most canned dog foods contain garlic because dogs like the taste.

Bookmark # 25-9

MAMMALS
Deer

- In most deer breeds, only male deer have antlers. Mature antlers are smooth and white like the bones in a skeleton because they are made of bone.
- Most deer shed their antlers each year. Growing antlers are covered in a soft fur called velvet.
- Male deer who fight have been known to lock antlers. If they can't separate themselves, the deer starve to death.
- Deer have been known to play a game like tag where the deer who's "it" tags another deer with its hooves.

8Bookmark # 25-8

MAMMALS
Cow

- About 8,500 years ago, cows were domesticated for milk, meat, their hides, and labor.
- A good milking cow produces almost 1,500 gallons of milk in a year or 14,640 pounds of milk.
- A herd of 60 cows can produce a ton of milk in one day.
- Cows tend to give more milk if they listen to music while being milked.

Bookmark # 25-7

SECTION VI: LIFE SCIENCES | 75

MAMMALS
Elephant

- An elephant has about 150,000 muscles in its trunk.
- Elephants don't drink through their trunks. They use their trunks to suck as much as three gallons of water to squirt in their mouths or over their backs.
- The longest elephant tusk on record was 10 feet long and weighed almost 230 pounds. African Elephant tusks average 6 to 8 feet long, and Asian Elephant tusks average about 5 feet.
- An elephant's leg bones are too close together to allow it to jump.
- Elephants from India are much easier to train than elephants from Africa.

MAMMALS
Giraffe

- Giraffes used to be called "cameleopards" because people thought they were a cross between a camel and a leopard.
- A giraffe's neck is about seven feet long, but has only seven bones—the same as a human.
- Giraffes' tongues average about 15 inches long.
- Giraffes sleep in stretches about four minutes long.
- A giraffe can run about 35 miles per hour. It could win a race with a horse and can usually outrun its enemies.
- A giraffe can go without water longer than a camel.

MAMMALS
Guinea Pig

- The Incas of Peru were the first to domesticate the guinea pig. They used the animals for food, as pets, and as sacrifices to the gods.
- Guinea pigs were first called pigs because the high-pitched squeal they make when they are frightened sounds like a pig.
- The name "guinea" may have originated when the small creatures that sounded like pigs were first taken to England, where they were sold for a gold coin called a guinea. Other possible origins are that Guineamen from the slave trade may have brought them to England or that "guinea" may be a corruption of the term *coney* (another small rodent).
- Guinea pigs have become popular as pets and as laboratory research animals.

MAMMALS
Hippopotamus

- A hippopotamus is a close relative of the pig.
- A hippo can weigh over 8,000 pounds. Only the elephant is a larger land mammal than the hippo.
- The skin of a hippo is so thick that most bullets can't pierce it. It is up to two inches thick.
- When a hippo is excited, working hard, or out of the water too long, it sweats red mucus through its skin.
- A hippopotamus that appears as if it's yawning near another hippo is actually asking for a fight.

MAMMALS
Horse

- Horses lock their legs into proper position to sleep standing up. Horses often don't lie down at all for a month or more at a time.
- A horse focuses its eyes by changing the angle of its head. A human's eye focuses by changing the shape of the lens within the eye.
- Horses are given shoes to keep their hooves from splitting.

MAMMALS
Kangaroo

- When Europeans first reached Australia in 1929, they asked what a certain animal was. The reply was "kangaroo," which meant "I don't know."
- The largest living species of kangaroos grow to be about 6.5 feet tall. An extinct species was more than 10 feet tall. Miniature kangaroos are about the size of a jackrabbit.
- Kangaroos use their tails for balance when they jump.
- Kangaroos are good swimmers. Someone once saw a kangaroo swimming more than a mile from shore.

Bookmark # 25-17

MAMMALS
Koala

- The koalas, sometimes called koala bears, of Australia aren't even remotely related to bears. They are related to kangaroos and opossums.
- The word *koala* means "one who doesn't drink." Koalas get most of their water from their only source of food: eucalyptus leaves.
- Koalas are becoming rare. They were first killed for their coats. Now, the destruction of eucalyptus forests threatens their habitat.

Bookmark # 25-18

MAMMALS
Lion

- A lion's roar can be heard for five miles. If an entire pride of lions roars at once, the sound causes the ground to shake.
- Female lions usually do the killing, but males are the first to eat.
- Lions make a kill only once every four or five times they try. A lion will kill about 20 large animals in a year.
- When a female lion goes out to hunt, another female will babysit the cubs and even nurse them. The babysitter gets a free meal for her services.

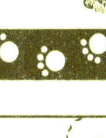

Bookmark # 25-19

MAMMALS
Moose

- A full-grown moose stands about eight feet high at the shoulder and weighs almost a ton. The antlers can span about five feet and weigh 50 pounds.
- Moose are so nearsighted they have mistaken cars as other moose.

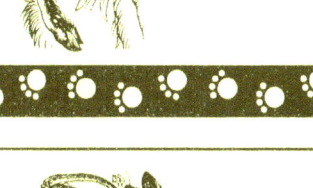

Bookmark # 25-20

MAMMALS
Platypus

- The duckbill platypus has fur like mammals, but lays eggs like birds.
- A baby platypus laps milk from the mother instead of sucking.
- The webbed toes of a platypus make it an excellent swimmer. The claws on the end of the toes are similar to those of a cat.
- The male platypus has a hollow claw or spur on each of its hind legs connected to a poison gland. He can poison his enemies by scratching them.
- A platypus can eat its own weight in worms in a day.

Bookmark # 25-21

SECTION VI: LIFE SCIENCES | 77

MAMMALS
Polar Bear

- The black nose of a polar bear can be seen through binoculars 6 miles away. Some people say the polar bear covers its nose with its paw while hunting to keep from being seen.
- Polar bears can smell a dead whale 20 miles or more away.
- Polar bears usually have no fear of humans. Polar bears have been known to stalk people and have even attacked large groups of hunters.

Bookmark # 25-22

MAMMALS
Porcupine

- Porcupines protect themselves by rolling into a ball so that only their quills are exposed.
- Each porcupine has about 30,000 quills.
- Porcupines don't throw their quills, but can make them stand on end and make them rattle.
- The hollow quills help keep porcupines afloat while they're swimming.

Bookmark # 25-23

MAMMALS
Skunk

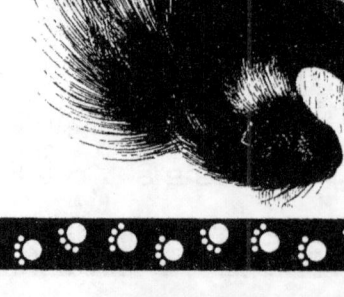

- Skunks, also called "polecats," come in spotted and striped varieties. One kind is striped like a zebra.
- The smelly oil that skunks spray from their anal glands is used to attract mates and ward off enemies. Humans can smell the spray at least a mile away.
- Skunks stamp their front feet as a warning before they spray.
- A skunk's spray can travel as far as 15 feet.
- A skunk can spray five to six times in a row.
- Skunks will not bite and spray at the same time.

Bookmark # 25-24

MAMMALS
Whale

- The blue whale is the largest animal ever—even larger than the dinosaurs were. The blue whale can be more than 100 feet long and weigh over 150 tons.
- No food a whale eats is over two inches long.
- A whale's heart beats only about nine times a minute.
- Whales can squeak, whistle, grunt, and click. The sounds they make can travel many miles.

Bookmark # 25-25

MAMMALS
Wolf

- Wolves live in closely-knit families. Wolves mate for life, sometimes with dogs. The pups from a wolf-dog cross are often vicious.
- Each wolf pack has its own territory covering 30 to 150 square miles in which they hunt.
- Wolves communicate by barking, growling, howling, and whimpering. Their howls can be heard up to 6 miles away. Contrary to popular belief, wolves don't howl at the moon.
- Father wolves often babysit the cubs while the mother hunts.

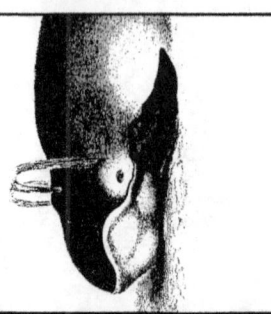

Bookmark # 25-26

BIRDS
Albatross

- Albatrosses are able to drink seawater. The water is filtered through a part of the body that can get rid of the salt.
- The wandering albatross of the Southern Hemisphere has a wingspan of nearly 12 feet.
- People once thought that the souls of dead men lived inside albatrosses.

Bookmark # 26-5

BIRDS
Types of Feathers

- down—small, very soft, fluffy feathers that protect the bird from extreme heat or cold
- contour—firm feathers, often downy near the base, that are the main body covering on the bird
- flight—larger feathers with strong stems found on the wings and tails of birds to help in flight; flight feathers are the ones used in making quill pens

Bookmark # 26-4

BIRDS
Feathers

- Feathers are made of keratin, the same substance that makes up human hair and nails.
- Hummingbirds can have fewer than 1,000 feathers, while a whistling swan can have over 25,000 feathers.
- Some birds bathe in water or dust to clean their feathers and to keep them free of parasites. Other birds sit near a smoking chimney to let the smoke drive parasites away.
- Feathers have been used for a variety of purposes, from decorations for hats to writing instruments to cleaning tools.

Bookmark # 26-3

BIRDS
Bird Nests

- Hummingbird nests can be as small as half a walnut shell. Eagles' nests can weigh more than four tons.
- Nests can be made of mud, straw, twigs, rocks, or other materials. Many birds like to include something shiny in their nests.
- Some birds, such as cuckoos and cowbirds, lay their eggs in a nest of another species. The other birds incubate and hatch the eggs.
- Some swallows and swifts use the sticky saliva they secrete to strengthen their nests. Some swifts' nests are cleaned and used in making birds' nest soup.

Bookmark # 26-2

BIRDS
Birds

- About 90% of extinct species are birds.
- Birds have fewer and lighter bones than other animals. Many bird bones have pockets of air connected directly to the lungs.
- Birds have no sense of smell.
- Birds use feathers for warmth and for flying.

Some characteristics of birds include having

- a backbone
- warm blood
- a covering of feathers except for the legs and feet
- scaly legs and feet
- wings instead of forelegs or arms

Bookmark # 26-1

SECTION VI: LIFE SCIENCES | 79

BIRDS

Bald Eagle

- Bald eagles aren't really bald. The small white feathers close to their heads simply make them look bald from a distance.
- Eagles can attack, kill, and carry an animal the size of a small deer.
- An average bald eagle's nest can weigh as much as 4,000 pounds, and be up to six feet in diameter and five feet high.
- The bald eagle is the national symbol of the United States.

Bookmark # 26-6

Chicken

- Christopher Columbus brought the first chicken to America.
- The world has about the same number of chickens as humans.
- Chickens are able to fly short distances at low altitudes.
- An average chicken lays five to seven eggs
- A hen will keep laying eggs only if the eggs are taken from her. Otherwise, she'll try to hatch the ones she has already laid.

Bookmark # 26-7

Flamingo

- Flamingoes aren't born pink. The color comes from eating tiny blue-green algae that turn pink during digestion.
- Flamingoes have openings on each side of their upper bills. The flamingo takes a beakful of water, then pumps out the water with the lower beak. A small amount of food is left behind for the flamingo to eat.
- A flamingo's knees bend backwards.

Bookmark # 26-8

Hummingbird

- The average hummingbird weighs less than a penny.
- Some hummingbirds are so small that they get caught in spider webs.
- Hummingbirds eat twice their body weight every day.
- Some species of hummingbirds can fly up to 700 miles per hour for short distances.
- Hummingbirds are the only birds than can fly backwards and can hover in the air.

Bookmark # 26-9

Kiwi Bird

- Kiwis are unable to fly.
- Kiwis are one of the few birds that are able to smell.
- The kiwi is the only bird that has poor eyesight. When a kiwi is out at night, it uses its beak to feel its way.
- The egg of the kiwi is about ½ the mother's weight. That would be like an average woman giving birth to a 30-pound baby (most babies are 7 to 8 pounds at birth).

Bookmark # 26-10

BOOKMARKS ACROSS THE CURRICULUM

AMPHIBIANS AND REPTILES

Amphibians

- About 4,000 different species of amphibians exist. They have the fewest number of species of the major animal groups.

- The word *amphibian* comes from the Greek word *amphibios*, which means "living two lives." Most amphibians live part of their lives in the water and part on land.

- Amphibians are cold-blooded creatures. Their body temperature corresponds to the temperature of their environment.

- Young amphibians look very different from adults (like tadpoles and frogs).

Bookmark # 27-1

BIRDS

Wild Turkey

- A turkey can grow to be four feet long and weigh more than 35 pounds.

- The only known use of the beard on a turkey is to tell the difference between male and female turkeys.

Bookmark # 26-14

BIRDS

Penguin

- All 18 species of penguins are native to the area south of the equator—most in Antarctica.

- Penguins can't fly, but are second only to the dolphin as the fastest swimmer in the ocean.

- Penguins are very loyal. Most have the same mate their entire lives. They will starve themselves so that their children can eat.

- The emperor penguin male is the one to sit on the egg up to four months. He doesn't eat at all during that time.

Bookmark # 26-13

BIRDS

Ostrich

- Ostriches are the largest birds in the world. The African ostrich can grow to eight feet tall and weigh well over 300 pounds.

- Although ostriches are too heavy to fly, they can run as fast as a horse, about 40 mph. Ostrich races with and without jockeys are held in South Africa.

- An eye of an ostrich is larger than its brain.

- One ostrich egg is about the same size as 24 chicken eggs.

Bookmark # 26-12

BIRDS

Loon

- Loons have difficulty getting off the ground to fly. Sometimes they have to flap their wings and "run" over the surface of the water a quarter of a mile before they can take off.

- Once they're in the air, loons can fly up to 60 miles per hour.

Bookmark # 26-11

SECTION VI: LIFE SCIENCES

AMPHIBIANS
Frog

- The tongue of frogs is attached at the front of the mouth to help them catch their prey. The sticky surface of the tongue holds the prey until it can be swallowed.
- Frogs have to close their eyes when they swallow because the eyeballs help push food down their throats.
- Some people consider frogs' legs a tasty treat.

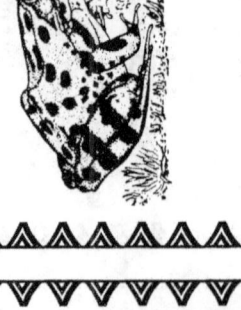

Bookmark # 27-6

AMPHIBIANS
Crocodile

- A crocodile weighing about 120 pounds can exert a force of about 1,540 pounds between its jaws. Humans can exert a pressure of about 40 to 80 pounds.
- Crocodiles are more dangerous in the water than they are on land because they can move faster and use their tails as weapons.
- Crocodiles don't chew their food, but swallow it whole. Small stones in their stomachs help grind the food.
- Plover birds act as toothbrushes and pick scraps of food from crocodiles' teeth.

Bookmark # 27-5

AMPHIBIANS
Chameleon

- Some species of chameleons can change color in response to temperature, light, or their emotions.
- A chameleon will take on the color of its environment even if it's completely blind.
- A chameleon becomes darker in sunlight.
- If a chameleon loses a fight, it hangs its head and turns dark green. If a chameleon is angry, it turns black.
- The eyes of a chameleon can move independently from one another.
- A chameleon's tongue is several inches longer than its body. It can catch insects 10 inches away.

Bookmark # 27-4

AMPHIBIANS AND REPTILES
Alligators and Crocodiles

Some differences between an alligator and a crocodile include

- Alligators are darker in color than crocodiles.
- An alligator's nose is broader and blunter than a crocodile's.
- You can see teeth on either side of the lower jaw when a crocodile's mouth is closed. An alligator's teeth are covered.
- Crocodiles are usually faster and more aggressive than alligators.

Bookmark # 27-3

AMPHIBIANS AND REPTILES
Reptiles

- About 7,000 species of reptiles exist. Some reptiles are alligators, crocodiles, lizards, snakes, and turtles.
- Reptiles are cold-blooded animals.
- Most reptiles lay eggs, although some have live births.
- Most reptiles have very short legs or no legs at all.
- Although some reptiles can hear, most don't have external ears.
- Most reptiles have dry, scaly skin.
- Reptiles often hibernate in both very cold and very hot weather.

Bookmark # 27-2

AMPHIBIANS AND REPTILES
Frogs & Toads

Some differences between frogs and toads include

- Toads have broader bodies and shorter, less powerful legs.
- A frog's skin is moist and sometimes slimy, while a toad's skin is dry to the touch.
- Toads are usually covered in warts, while frogs usually have smooth skin.
- Frogs are often greenish in color, while toads are usually brown or gray.

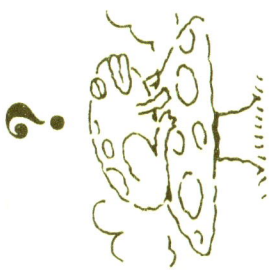

Bookmark # 27-7

AMPHIBIANS AND REPTILES
Snake

- Snakes don't have ears. Their flicking tongues help to pick up sound vibrations instead of hearing the way humans do.
- The underbelly of a snake feels smooth when rubbed one way and rough when rubbed the other.
- Snakes have no eyelids, so their eyes are always open. They can't focus on an unmoving object, but can see movement.
- Some kinds of snakes can go an entire year without having to eat.
- In 1912, a reticulated python 33 feet long was found in Indonesia.

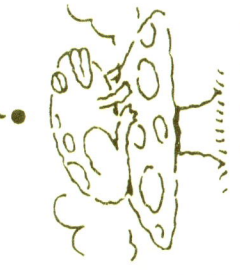

Bookmark # 27-8

CRUSTACEANS AND MOLLUSKS
Crustaceans

- The word *crustacean* comes from a Latin word meaning "hard shell." Instead of a skeleton, crustaceans have hard shells to protect their soft bodies.
- Most crustaceans have many jointed legs. Some crustaceans are able to grow a new limb if one is lost in an accident.
- Some types of crustaceans are barnacles, crabs, crayfish, lobsters, shrimp, water fleas, and wood lice.

Bookmark # 28-1

CRUSTACEANS AND MOLLUSKS
Mollusks

- Mollusks usually have shells instead of backbones. The shell is on the outside of some mollusks, such as snails. The shell is inside some mollusks, such as octopuses.
- A mollusk is symmetrical with nearly identical features on each side of an imaginary line drawn down its middle.
- Mollusks have a muscular foot they use for digging, swimming, or moving on land.
- Clams, mussels, scallops, slugs, and whelks are some types of mollusks.

Bookmark # 28-2

CRUSTACEANS AND MOLLUSKS
Barnacle

- Barnacles are crustaceans that attach themselves to anything—docks, rocks, boats, and even whales. They stay attached to the same object their entire lives.
- Barnacles that attach themselves to a ship's hull can interfere with a ship's movement. The barnacles have to be removed to save fuel.
- When they are born, barnacles look like water fleas. In their next stage of development, they have three eyes and 12 legs. In their third stage of development, they have no eyes and 24 legs.

Bookmark # 28-3

SECTION VI: LIFE SCIENCES | 83

CRUSTACEANS AND MOLLUSKS

Lobster

- Lobsters have 10 legs, 8 for walking and the 2 large claws.
- American lobsters can move through the water at a rate of 25 feet per second or more than 17 miles per hour.
- A lobster can lay 100,000 eggs at a time, but most are eaten by predators.
- Lobsters feel pain when boiled alive. Soaking them in salt water before cooking lessens the pain.

Bookmark # 28-4

CRUSTACEANS AND MOLLUSKS

Octopus

- The blood of an octopus is blue because it contains oxygen-carrying copper molecules that create the blue color.
- The color of an octopus can change from gray or green to pink among rocks or seaweed. If an octopus gets angry, it may become a dark red. It also squirts black ink and gets away when the attacker can't see through the cloud.

Bookmark # 28-5

CRUSTACEANS AND MOLLUSKS

Oysters and Pearls

- A natural pearl forms when a foreign object such as a grain of sand enters an oyster shell. The oyster covers the foreign material with a hard material called nacre. Eventually layers of nacre form a pearl.
- Cultured pearls are formed when a small piece of shell is surgically placed in the oyster to force the secretion of the nacre.
- Artificial pearls are usually made of hollow glass lined with fish scales to produce the look of natural pearls.
- Pollution and predators are threatening oyster beds.

Bookmark # 28-6

CRUSTACEANS AND MOLLUSKS

Shells

Shells are the homes or outside skeletons of mollusks. Over 100,000 different kinds of shells exist. Some types of shells are

- shiny and pearly shells called jingle shells
- smooth shells such as those of mussels and clams
- ribbed shells such as those of scallops
- spiral shells such as those of snails

Bookmark # 28-7

CRUSTACEANS AND MOLLUSKS

Snail

- Snails' teeth are arranged in rows along their tongues. The teeth are used like a file to saw or cut through food.
- Snails are deaf.
- A snail mates only once in its entire life.
- The slipper-shell snails are all born males and turn into females at a later age.
- A snail native to Africa can be over nine inches long and weigh more than a pound.
- Snails are attracted to the scent of beer.

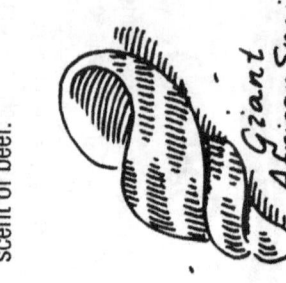

Giant African Snail

Bookmark # 28-8

84 BOOKMARKS ACROSS THE CURRICULUM

INSECTS
Insects

- If the name of every species of insect were listed in a book, the book would have to be about 6,000 pages long to hold the names of the five million different species known.
- More insects can be found in one square mile of rural land than there are humans on Earth.
- The total weight of insects on Earth is about 12 times more than the total weight of humans.

Bookmark # 29-1

INSECTS
Ant

- An ant can lift about 50 times its own weight. That would be like a human lifting a four-ton truck or a small elephant.
- About 10,000 average-sized ants weigh about the same as an average-sized man.
- An ant doesn't always die right away if it loses its head. Ants are able to stay alive because they don't have spinal cords.
- Ants wash themselves 15 to 20 times a day.

Bookmark # 29-2

INSECTS
Bee

- Bees travel a total of 50,000 to 90,000 miles to make one pound of honey.
- When bees hatch, they are fully-grown.
- When temperatures are very hot, bees flap their wings in the hive to keep the wax from melting.
- Bees do a "round dance" to tell other bees how far to go for food. Their "waggle dance" tells other bees the direction to go.

Bookmark # 29-3

INSECTS
Beetle

- Earth has more beetles than any other living creature. Nearly 250,000 different species of beetles exist. About 28,000 different species of beetles can be found in the United States.
- Goliath beetles are the heaviest insects on Earth; they can weigh about a quarter pound. They have been known to break windows if they fly against them.
- Wood beetles knock their heads against wood if something disturbs them.
- One half of each of a whirligig beetle's eyes looks up, while the other half looks down.

Bookmark # 29-4

INSECTS
Butterfly

- More than 100,000 different species of moths exist, but there are only about 18,500 species of butterflies.
- The colors on a butterfly come from tiny scales on the wings.
- Many butterflies migrate south for the winter the way birds do.
- Butterflies taste with their feet.
- A butterfly knows water has sugar in it if only one teaspoon of sugar is dissolved in nearly 400 gallons of water.
- Some butterflies sip the juice of rotten fruit. The juices contain alcohol and sometimes a butterfly can become too drunk to fly.

Bookmark # 29-5

SECTION VI: LIFE SCIENCES | 85

INSECTS

Fly

- Flies can beat their wings up to 10,000 times a minute. The movement of the wings causes the buzzing sound flies make.
- A fly can travel up to 50 miles per hour for a short distance, but rarely goes more than 10 miles from where it was hatched.
- Each leg on a fly has small suction cups to help it walk up a wall and even on the ceiling.
- A pair of houseflies can produce as many as 325,923,200,000,000 offspring and their descendants in one summer.

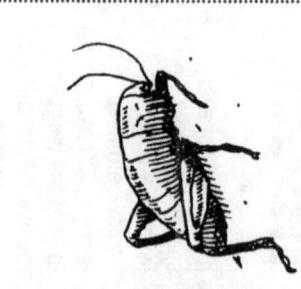

INSECTS

Flea

- A flea's life span is about two and one-half years.
- A flea can jump about 18 inches high and 13 inches across. If humans had that skill, they could easily achieve a 600-foot broad jump and 360-foot high jump.
- Snow fleas in the Himalayas freeze solid at night and thaw the next day without harm.

INSECTS

Firefly

- Fireflies, also called "glowworms" or "lightning bugs," are actually beetles, not flies. Several different species are known.
- The light from a firefly comes from an area on the sides of its stomach. Six substances in the fatty tissue mix with oxygen to make the glow.
- Fireflies are most active at night.

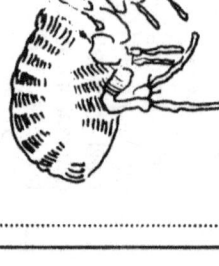

INSECTS

Dragonfly

- Dragonflies in several different brilliant colors have been around at least 320 million years.
- Dragonflies spend several years living underwater as nymphs before they become adults, then live about one day.
- Dragonflies have over 20,000 lenses in each eye to help draw the light into the eye. Humans have only one lens in each eye.

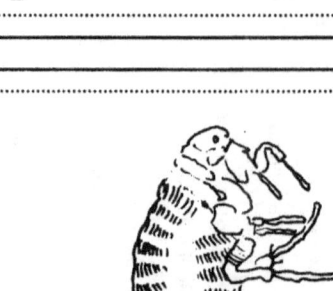

INSECTS

Cricket

- A cricket's legs are made of a hard substance almost like fingernails in a human.
- Crickets' ears are located on their knees.
- Only male crickets chirp. They make the sound by rubbing their legs together.
- If you count the number of cricket chirps you hear in 15 seconds, then add 40, you'll know the temperature in degrees Fahrenheit.

INSECTS

Grasshopper

- Grasshoppers can jump over obstacles 500 times their own height. That's like a person jumping about 3,000 feet high.
- Grasshoppers can jump 20 times their body length. A man would have to jump about 120 feet to match that skill.
- A bird watcher in Costa Rica once thought he'd discovered a new species of bird, but it turned out to be a large grasshopper.

Bookmark # 29-11

INSECTS

Mosquito

- Mosquitoes move their wings about 1,000 times a second.
- Only the female mosquito buzzes and bites. She can absorb one and one-half times her own weight in blood at one time.
- The itching and bump from a mosquito bite is from an allergic reaction to mosquito saliva.
- Mosquitoes are attracted to the color blue twice as much as to any other color.
- Mosquitoes have been found near the North Pole.

Bookmark # 29-12

INSECTS

Moth

- Moths have been around for at least 140 million years. They were alive at the time of the dinosaurs.
- Moths have hairy bodies to keep them warm when they fly on cold nights.
- Moths use the Moon and the Sun to find their way. They keep the light in front of them to fly straight. Moths flutter around light bulbs because they can't tell the difference between the Moon and the bulb.
- Some moths don't have mouths. They don't eat at all, but survive on energy stored up when they were caterpillars.

Bookmark # 29-13

INSECTS

Roach

- Roaches have been around for at least 280 million years. They haven't changed in any way for at least 250 million years.
- About 4,000 different species of roaches exist.
- Roaches "hear" with their bellies.
- A roach can live several weeks after its head is gone.
- When a roach dies, its legs stiffen. The roach falls on its side, then rolls onto its back.

Bookmark # 29-14

INSECTS

Termite

- Although termites look a little like ants, they are actually a part of the cockroach family.
- Termites have a life span of more than 25 years. The queen can live about 50 years.
- The termite queen is 500 times larger than the termite king, or 20,000 times larger than a worker.
- The termite queen lays an egg about every three seconds of her life—about 30,000 eggs per day.
- A colony of 60,000 termites will eat about an ounce of wood every five days.
- Some breeds of termites will build eaves onto their nests to keep out the rain.

Bookmark # 29-15

SECTION VI: LIFE SCIENCES

MISCELLANEOUS ANIMALS

Arachnids

- Arachnids include creatures such as mites, scorpions, spiders, and ticks. The horseshoe crab is actually an arachnid, not a crab (crabs are crustaceans).
- Arachnids have a hard protective coating called an exoskeleton on their bodies.
- Some arachnids can live without food for over a year.
- Because it has 6 joints on each of its 8 legs, a spider has 48 knees.
- Spiders taste with their feet.

Bookmark # 30-1

MISCELLANEOUS ANIMALS

Earthworm

- Earthworms can pull 10 times their own weight.
- About three million earthworms can be found in one acre of fertile soil.
- Earthworms usually range in size from 1/25 inch to over a foot in length, but some tropical species grow to 11 feet long.
- An earthworm can have as many as 10 hearts.
- Earthworms don't have lungs; they breathe through their skin.
- Earthworms eat dirt, use the nutrients from it, and pass grains of soil out of their bodies. An earthworm will pass one-half pound of soil through its body in one day.

Bookmark # 30-2

MISCELLANEOUS ANIMALS

Echinoderms

- An echinoderm is an organism that has no backbone, but does have an outside skeleton.
- Echinoderms have symmetrical bodies, often with five identical sections.
- Echinoderms usually live in or near the ocean.
- Sea cucumbers, sea urchins, and starfish are examples of echinoderms.

Bookmark # 30-3

MISCELLANEOUS ANIMALS

Fish

- About 25,000 recognized species of fish exist, in colors from yellow to red to blue and many others. The size of fish ranges from a fraction of an inch for guppies to over 40 feet for the giant whale shark.
- Fish use gills instead of lungs to breathe.
- Fish can't see very well, but can hear.
- Most fish are constantly in motion, but have less active times. Some fish sleep by standing on their tails or leaning against rocks.
- A goldfish has a memory span of only three seconds.

Bookmark # 30-4

MISCELLANEOUS ANIMALS

Invertebrates

- About 99% of the world's animals are invertebrates.
- Invertebrates are animals without a backbone or an internal skeleton. Sometimes invertebrates have a hard shell or other outer coating to protect them.
- Some single-celled invertebrates have characteristics similar to plants.
- Invertebrates aren't very intelligent. Very few are able to be taught to avoid dangerous places.
- Some types of invertebrates are arachnids, echinoderms, insects, mollusks, protozoa, sponges, and worms.

Bookmark # 30-5

88 | BOOKMARKS ACROSS THE CURRICULUM

MISCELLANEOUS ANIMALS

Jellyfish

- Jellyfish, also known as medusas, are made up of 99% water.
- The colors of jellyfish include pale blue, purple, and red, as well as being transparent.
- If left in the sun too long, jellyfish can start to look like spilled jelly.
- Jellyfish move by jet propulsion. They pull water into their bodies, then force it back out. The water moves in one direction and the jellyfish in the opposite direction.
- The skin of the pyrosoma jellyfish works like a lighted billboard if a design is traced on its skin.

MISCELLANEOUS ANIMALS

Sea Horse

- Sea horses spend much of their time with their tails wrapped around seaweed.
- A female sea horse gives her eggs to the male. He incubates them in his brood pouch until they hatch.
- About 300 baby sea horses are born at a time, but few reach adulthood. Most are eaten—some of them by their own father.

MISCELLANEOUS ANIMALS

Sharks

- Sharks have to keep moving or they'll suffocate. Water has to move across their gills to give them oxygen.
- A shark is the only fish that can blink with both eyes.
- Nearly two-thirds of a shark's brain is used for the sense of smell.
- Sharks have no bones. Instead, they have cartilage to help them move more easily through the water.
- The teeth of a tiger shark are on a spring. When the shark's mouth is closed, the teeth are pressed back against the gums. When the shark's mouth is open, the teeth spring out.

MISCELLANEOUS ANIMALS

Starfish

- Most starfish have 5 arms, but some have more than 40.
- Starfish are meat-eaters that feed mostly on mollusks and crustaceans.
- A starfish is the only animal that can turn its stomach inside out. It does this to let digestive juices break down its food.
- Most starfish can grow a new arm if one is damaged or completely severed. Some starfish can reproduce their whole bodies from a single piece only a half-inch long.
- Starfish can't hear.

SECTION VI: LIFE SCIENCES

Section VII

Important People

PRESIDENTS

★★★
George Washington
(1732-1799)
1st President

Term—1789 to 1797

First Lady—Martha Dandridge Custis Washington

Vice President—John Adams

Political Party—none

Home State—Virginia

Career—surveyor

Fun Facts

- Two of Washington's horses were killed as he rode them; the bullets pierced Washington's hat and coat, but didn't harm him.
- Washington danced with every woman at the inaugural ball.
- The story of Washington chopping down a cherry tree is likely not true.

★★★

Bookmark # 31-1

PRESIDENTS

★★★
John Adams
(1735-1826)
2nd President

Term—1797 to 1801

First Lady—Abigail Smith Adams

Vice President—Thomas Jefferson

Political Party—Federalist

Home State—Massachusetts

Career—lawyer, diplomat in Europe

Fun Facts

- Adams was instrumental in getting the Declaration of Independence passed.
- John and Abigail Adams were the first to live in the White House (then called "Presidential Palace"). Abigail hung her laundry in an unfinished room.

★★★

Bookmark # 31-2

PRESIDENTS

★★★
Thomas Jefferson
(1743-1826)
3rd President

Term—1801 to 1809

First Lady—Martha Wayles Skelton Jefferson

Vice Presidents—Aaron Burr and George Clinton

Political Party—Democratic-Republican

Home State—Virginia

Career—farmer, lawyer

Fun Facts

- Jefferson was also an inventor and architect.
- The money system of dollars and cents started with Jefferson.
- Jefferson was very casual and often wore slippers when greeting guests.

★★★

Bookmark # 31-3

SECTION VII: IMPORTANT PEOPLE | 91

PRESIDENTS

★★ JAMES MADISON
(1751-1836)
4th President

Term—1809 to 1817

First Lady—Dolley Payne Todd Madison

Vice Presidents—Elbridge Gerry and George Clinton

Political Party—Democratic-Republican

Home State—Virginia

Career—planter, statesman, lawyer

Fun Facts
- Madison's nickname was "Father of the Constitution."
- Madison led the United States into the War of 1812 and barely escaped when the British burned the White House.
- At five feet four inches tall, Madison was the shortest president.

Bookmark # 31-4

PRESIDENTS

★★ JAMES MONROE
(1735-1826)
5th President

Term—1817 to 1825

First Lady—Elizabeth Kortright Monroe

Vice President—Daniel D. Tompkins

Political Party—Democratic-Republican

Home State—Virginia

Career—lawyer

Fun Facts
- The Monroe Doctrine was a warning to Europe to seek no more colonies in the New World.
- Monroe crossed the Delaware River with George Washington.
- A bullet hit Monroe in the shoulder while he fought at Trenton.

Bookmark # 31-5

PRESIDENTS

★★ JOHN QUINCY ADAMS
(1767-1848)
6th President

Term—1825 to 1829

First Lady—Louisa Catherine Johnson Adams

Vice President—John C. Calhoun

Political Party—Democratic-Republican

Home State—Massachusetts

Career—lawyer, statesman

Fun Facts
- John Quincy Adams was the son of John Adams, the second president.
- The nickname of Adams was "Old Man Eloquent," although he had a very stern manner.
- Adams tried to get slavery abolished.

Bookmark # 31-6

PRESIDENTS

★★ ANDREW JACKSON
(1767-1845)
7th President

Term—1829 to 1837

First Lady—Rachel Donelson Robards Jackson

Vice Presidents—John C. Calhoun and Martin Van Buren

Political Party—Democratic

Home State—Tennessee

Career—lawyer, soldier, planter

Fun Facts
- Jackson's nickname was "Old Hickory."
- Jackson became a Revolutionary War soldier at age 13. He was taken prisoner and, after refusing to clean a British officer's boots, received a saber blow to the forehead, which left a scar.

Bookmark # 31-7

PRESIDENTS

★★ MARTIN VAN BUREN
(1782-1862)
8th President

Term—1837 to 1841

First Lady—Hannah Hoes Van Buren

Vice President—Richard M. Johnson

Political Party—Democratic

Home State—New York

Career—lawyer

Fun Facts
- Van Buren's nickname was "Little Magician" for his skill in politics.
- Van Buren was the first president to serve only one term because voters thought he spent too much money.

Bookmark # 31-8

PRESIDENTS

WILLIAM HENRY HARRISON
(1773-1841)
9th President

Term—one month in 1841

First Lady—Anna Tuthill Symmes Harrison

Vice President—John Tyler

Political Party—Whig

Home State—Ohio

Career—farmer, soldier

Fun Facts
- "Tippecanoe and Tyler too" for his nickname and running mate was Harrison's campaign slogan.
- Harrison's father was one of the men who signed the Declaration of Independence.
- Harrison died of pneumonia after riding in the inauguration parade without his hat or coat.

Bookmark # 31-9

PRESIDENTS

JOHN TYLER
(1790-1862)
10th President

Term—1841 to 1845

First Ladies—Letitia Christian Tyler and Julia Gardiner Tyler

Vice President—none

Political Party—Whig

Home State—Virginia

Career—lawyer, governor

Fun Facts
- Tyler was the first vice president to reach office on the death of the president.
- Tyler was the first president to marry while in the White House. His first wife died in 1842, and he married his second wife in 1844. Tyler had 15 children.

Bookmark # 31-10

PRESIDENTS

JAMES KNOX POLK
(1795-1849)
11th President

Term—1845 to 1849

First Lady—Sara Childress Polk

Vice President—George M. Dallas

Political Party—Democratic

Home State—Tennessee

Career—lawyer

Fun Facts
- Polk was the first presidential candidate that few people knew about before his campaign.
- Polk accomplished almost everything he promised during his campaign.

Bookmark # 31-11

PRESIDENTS

ZACHARY TAYLOR
(1784-1850)
12th President

Term—1849 to 1850 (16 months)

First Lady—Margaret Mackall Smith Taylor

Vice President—Millard Fillmore

Political Party—Whig

Home State—Louisiana

Career—soldier

Fun Facts
- Taylor's nickname was "Old Rough and Ready."
- Taylor spent 40 years as a soldier and was a hero in the war with Mexico.
- Taylor's death occurred five days after suffering sunstroke while dedicating the Washington Monument.

Bookmark # 31-12

PRESIDENTS

MILLARD FILLMORE
(1800-1874)
13th President

Term—1850 to 1853

First Lady—Abigail Powers Fillmore

Vice President—None

Political Party—Whig

Home State—New York

Career—lawyer

Fun Facts
- Fillmore was the last Whig to serve as president.
- Although Fillmore was antislavery, he signed the Fugitive Slave Act to force runaway slaves back South. He tried to work out a compromise on issues.
- Fillmore was self-educated.

Bookmark # 31-13

PRESIDENTS

★★★ Franklin Pierce
(1804-1869)
14th President

Term—1853 to 1857

First Lady—Jane Means Appleton Pierce

Vice President—William R. D. King

Political Party—Democratic

Home State—New Hampshire

Career—lawyer

Fun Facts

- Pierce was from the North, but favored the South politically.
- The war secretary under Pierce was Jefferson Davis, who later became the Confederate president.
- Pierce started the tradition of having a Christmas tree in the White House.

Bookmark # 31-14

PRESIDENTS

★★★ James Buchanan
(1791-1868)
15th President

Term—1857 to 1861

First Lady—Harriet Lane (Buchanan's niece, who served as hostess because Buchanan was a bachelor)

Vice President—John C. Breckinridge

Political Party—Democratic

Home State—Pennsylvania

Career—lawyer

Fun Facts

- Buchanan's efforts delayed the start of the Civil War.
- Buchanan was the only president who never married. He was once engaged to Ann Coleman, but she died before they could be married.

Bookmark # 31-15

PRESIDENTS

★★★ Abraham Lincoln
(1809-1865)
16th President

Term—1861 to 1865

First Lady—Mary Todd Lincoln

Vice Presidents—Hannibal Hamlin and Andrew Johnson

Political Party—Republican

Home State—Illinois

Career—lawyer

Fun Facts

- Lincoln was the first Republican president.
- Lincoln and Stephen A. Douglas were rivals, first for marriage with Mary Todd (Lincoln won), then over a Senate seat (Douglas won).
- At six feet four inches tall, Lincoln was the tallest president.

Bookmark # 31-16

PRESIDENTS

★★★ Andrew Johnson
(1808-1875)
17th President

Term—1865 to 1869

First Lady—Eliza McCardle Johnson

Vice President—none

Political Party—Democrat-National Union

Home State—Tennessee

Career—tailor, public official

Fun Facts

- Johnson was accused of misconduct of office and came one vote short of being "fired" as president.
- Johnson's wife taught him how to read.
- People sometimes called Johnson a "drunkard" or "touched with insanity."

Bookmark # 31-17

PRESIDENTS

★★★ Ulysses Simpson Grant
(1822-1885)
18th President

Term—1869 to 1877

First Lady—Julia Dent Grant

Vice Presidents—Schuyler Colfax and Henry Wilson

Political Party—Republican

Home State—Illinois

Career—soldier

Fun Facts

- Grant was a Civil War hero. After General Robert E. Lee surrendered, Grant allowed Lee's men to keep their horses for farm work.

Bookmark # 31-18

---

94 | BOOKMARKS ACROSS THE CURRICULUM

PRESIDENTS

★★★
RUTHERFORD BIRCHARD HAYES
(1822-1893)
19th President

Term—1877 to 1881

First Lady—Lucy Ware Webb Hayes

Vice President—William A. Wheeler

Political Party—Republican

Home State—Ohio

Career—lawyer

Fun Facts
- Samuel J. Tilden, the Democratic candidate, said dishonest elections in the South allowed Hayes to win.

Bookmark # 31-19

PRESIDENTS

★★★
JAMES ABRAM GARFIELD
(1831-1881)
20th President

Term—1881 (6½ months)

First Lady—Lucretia Rudolph Garfield

Vice President—Chester A. Arthur

Political Party—Republican

Home State—Ohio

Career—lawyer

Fun Facts
- For a time, Garfield was the youngest Union general in the Civil War.
- Charles Guiteau, who ran for office and lost, assassinated Garfield.

Bookmark # 31-20

PRESIDENTS

★★★
CHESTER ALAN ARTHUR
(1829-1885)
21st and 24th President

Term—1881 to 1885

First Lady—Mary Arthur McElory (Arthur's sister, who acted as hostess)

Vice President—none

Political Party—Republican

Home State—New York

Career—teacher, lawyer

Fun Facts
- Arthur's wife, Ellen Lewis Herndon Arthur, died the year before he became president.
- Arthur dressed so well that his nickname was "Elegant Arthur."
- While in office, Arthur held a rummage sale of items from the White House attic.

Bookmark # 31-21

PRESIDENTS

★★★
GROVER CLEVELAND
(1837-1908)
22nd President

Terms—1885 to 1889 and 1893 to 1897

First Lady—Frances Folsom Cleveland

Vice Presidents—Thomas A. Hendricks and Adlai E. Stevenson

Political Party—Democratic

Home State—New York

Career—lawyer

Fun Facts
- Cleveland is the only president so far to have been elected to nonconsecutive terms.
- Cleveland's daughter Ruth is the only president's child to be born during the term of office. Actually, she was born in 1891, between his two terms in office. The Baby Ruth candy bar is named for her.

Bookmark # 31-22

PRESIDENTS

★★★
BENJAMIN HARRISON
(1833-1901)
23rd President

Term—1889 to 1893

First Lady—Caroline Lavina Scott Harrison

Vice President—Levi P. Morton

Political Party—Republican

Home State—Indiana

Career—lawyer

Fun Facts
- Harrison was the grandson of William Henry Harrison, the ninth president.

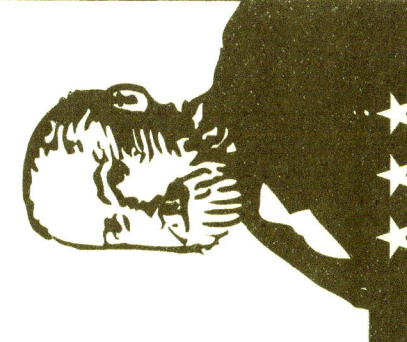

Bookmark # 31-23

SECTION VII: IMPORTANT PEOPLE | 95

PRESIDENTS

WILLIAM McKINLEY
(1843-1901)
25th President

Term—1897 to 1901

First Lady—Ida Saxton McKinley

Vice Presidents—Garret A. Hobart and Theodore Roosevelt

Political Party—Republican

Home State—Ohio

Career—lawyer

Fun Facts

- Although McKinley refused to leave his sickly wife to campaign, he still won the election.
- McKinley once tried to stop people from attacking a man who had just tried to kill him.

Bookmark # 31-24

PRESIDENTS

THEODORE ROOSEVELT
(1858-1919)
26th President

Term—1901 to 1909

First Lady—Edith Kermit Carow Roosevelt

Vice President—Charles W. Fairbanks

Political Party—Republican

Home State—New York

Career—lawyer, public official

Fun Facts

- Because Roosevelt liked the area, he created Theodore Roosevelt National Park in North Dakota.

Bookmark # 31-25

PRESIDENTS

WILLIAM HOWARD TAFT
(1857-1930)
27th President

Term—1909 to 1913

First Lady—Helen Herron Taft

Vice President—James S. Sherman

Political Party—Republican

Home State—Ohio

Career—lawyer

Fun Facts

- Near the end of his life, Taft was Chief Justice of the Supreme Court. He preferred that job to being president.
- Taft weighed between 300 and 350 pounds. He had a special bathtub big enough for him installed at the White House.

Bookmark # 31-26

PRESIDENTS

WOODROW WILSON
(1856-1924)
28th President

Term—1913 to 1921

First Ladies—Ellen Louise Axson Wilson and Edith Bolling Galt Wilson

Vice President—Thomas R. Marshall

Political Party—Democratic

Home State—New Jersey

Career—educator, lawyer

Fun Facts

- Part of the reason Wilson won the election was because votes were split between Taft and Roosevelt.
- Wilson's efforts at trying to keep the United States out of World War I earned him the 1920 Nobel Peace Prize.

Bookmark # 31-27

PRESIDENTS

WARREN GAMALIEL HARDING
(1856-1923)
29th President

Term—1921 to 1923

First Lady—Florence Kling Harding

Vice President—Calvin Coolidge

Political Party—Republican

Home State—Ohio

Career—editor

Fun Facts

- Harding won the election with a landslide victory.
- Many scandals followed Harding's death, even though he had many trusted friends helping him with his work.
- Harding organized the Citizen's Cornet Band. The band played for both Republican and Democratic rallies.

Bookmark # 31-28

PRESIDENTS

★★ John Calvin Coolidge
(1872-1933)
30th President

Term—1923 to 1929

First Lady—Grace Anna Goodhue Coolidge

Vice President—Charles G. Dawes

Political Party—Republican

Home State—Massachusetts

Career—lawyer

Fun Facts

- Coolidge's nickname was "Silent Cal" because he was known for speaking as little as possible.

Bookmark # 31-29

PRESIDENTS

★★ Herbert Clark Hoover
(1874-1964)
31st President

Term—1929 to 1933

First Lady—Lou Henry Hoover

Vice President—Charles Curtis

Political Party—Republican

Home State—California

Career—engineer

Fun Facts

- Hoover was orphaned at an early age and raised by Quakers.
- Hoover's famous promise was to put "a chicken in every pot."

Bookmark # 31-30

PRESIDENTS

★★ Franklin Delano Roosevelt
(1882-1945)
32nd President

Term—1933 to 1945

First Lady—Anna Eleanor Roosevelt

Vice Presidents—John N. Garner, Henry A. Wallace, and Harry S. Truman

Political Party—Democratic

Home State—New York

Career—farmer, lawyer, public official

Fun Facts

- Infantile paralysis forced Roosevelt to walk with braces or use a wheelchair.
- Roosevelt's "fireside chats" on radio were famous, and he was the first president to appear on television.

Bookmark # 31-31

PRESIDENTS

★★ Harry S Truman
(1884-1972)
33rd President

Term—1945 to 1953

First Lady—Elizabeth Virginia Wallace Truman

Vice President—Alben W. Barkley

Political Party—Democratic

Home State—Missouri

Career—farmer, businessperson, public official

Fun Facts

- The *S* in Truman's name doesn't stand for any name; his complete middle name is simply "*S*".

Bookmark # 31-32

PRESIDENTS

★★ Dwight David Eisenhower
(1890-1969)
34th President

Term—1953 to 1961

First Lady—Mamie Geneva Doud Eisenhower

Vice President—Richard M. Nixon

Political Party—Republican

Home State—Kansas

Career—soldier

Fun Facts

- Eisenhower was a five-star general in the military.
- Eisenhower directed the invasion of Europe that led to Germany's surrender in World War II.
- While serving as president, Eisenhower suffered a mild stroke.

Bookmark # 31-33

SECTION VII: IMPORTANT PEOPLE | 97

PRESIDENTS

John Fitzgerald Kennedy
(1917-1963)
35th President

Term—1961 to 1963

First Lady—Jacqueline Lee Bouvier Kennedy

Vice President—Lyndon B. Johnson

Political Party—Democratic

Home State—Massachusetts

Career—congressman, senator

Fun Facts

- An injured back during a World War II sea battle became a life-long problem for Kennedy.
- Kennedy's book *Profiles in Courage* won the Pulitzer Prize for biography in 1957.
- Kennedy established the Peace Corps.

Bookmark # 31-34

PRESIDENTS

Lyndon Baines Johnson
(1908-1973)
36th President

Term—1963 to 1969

First Lady—Claudia Taylor Johnson

Vice President—Hubert H. Humphrey

Political Party—Democratic

Home State—Texas

Career—rancher, congressman, senator

Fun Facts

- Johnson was the first member of Congress to enlist in the armed forces after the attack on Pearl Harbor.
- Johnson won his election by a record-breaking nearly 16 million votes. He declined to seek another term because he didn't like the escalating problems with Vietnam.

Bookmark # 31-35

PRESIDENTS

Richard Milhous Nixon
(1913-1994)
37th President

Term—1969 to 1974

First Lady—Patricia Ryan Nixon

Vice Presidents—Spiro T. Agnew and Gerald R. Ford

Political Party—Republican

Home States—New York and California

Career—congressman, senator

Fun Facts

- Nixon was the first president to resign from office to avoid impeachment.
- Nixon's famous quotation is "I am not a crook."

Bookmark # 31-36

PRESIDENTS

Gerald Randolph Ford
(1913-)
38th President

Term—1974 to 1977

First Lady—Elizabeth Bloomer Ford

Vice President—Nelson A. Rockefeller

Political Party—Republican

Home State—Michigan

Career—lawyer, congressman

Fun Facts

- Ford is the only president never to have been elected. He became president when Nixon resigned, then lost the election to Carter.
- Ford was known for his frequent vetoes because the Democrats had a majority in Congress.

Bookmark # 31-37

PRESIDENTS

James Earl Carter, Jr.
(1924-)
39th President

Term—1977 to 1981

First Lady—Rosalynn Smith Carter

Vice President—Walter F. Mondale

Political Party—Democratic

Home State—Georgia

Career—peanut farmer, governor

Fun Facts

- Although his first name is "James," Carter prefers to be called "Jimmy."
- Carter is active in the charity Habitat for Humanity.

Bookmark # 31-38

98 | BOOKMARKS ACROSS THE CURRICULUM

EXPLORERS

Vasco De Balboa
(1890-1969)

- Vasco de Balboa was born in Jerez de los Caballeros, Spain.
- Balboa once ran a plantation, but was so far in debt, he fled his creditors by hiding in a cask aboard a supply ship.
- Balboa asked King Ferdinand II for an army to find and conquer a rich land rumored to be south of Panama. The king agreed, but asked Pedrarias Davila to be governor. Balboa set out on his own and discovered the Pacific Ocean. He was arrested by Pedrarias Davila in 1519, convicted of treason, and beheaded.

Bookmark # 32-1

PRESIDENTS

George Walker Bush
(1946-)
43rd President

Term—2001 to present

First Lady—Laura Welch Bush

Vice President—Richard B. Cheney

Political Party—Republican

Home State—Texas

Career—business person, politician

Fun Facts

- Bush is the son of George Herbert Walker Bush, the 41st president.
- Bush was once part owner of the Texas Rangers baseball team. He preferred sitting with the fans to sitting in the owner's box.

Bookmark # 31-42

PRESIDENTS

William Jefferson Clinton
(1946-)
42nd President

Term—1993 to 2001

First Lady—Hillary Rodham Clinton

Vice President—Albert A. Gore, Jr.

Political Party—Democratic

Home State—Arkansas

Career—educator, attorney, and politician

Fun Facts

- Clinton's blood father, William Jefferson Blythe, was killed in an automobile accident before Clinton was born.
- Clinton planned to be a doctor until he met President Kennedy on a Boys' Nation trip to Washington.

Bookmark # 31-41

PRESIDENTS

George Herbert Walker Bush
(1924-)
41st President

Term—1989 to 1993

First Lady—Barbara Pierce Bush

Vice President—J. Danforth Quayle

Political Party—Republican

Home State—Texas

Career—businessperson in the oil industry, politician

Fun Facts

- During World War II, Bush was the U.S. Navy's youngest fighter pilot.
- Bush was captain of the baseball team while he attended Yale.
- Bush is a former director of the CIA.

Bookmark # 31-40

PRESIDENTS

Ronald Wilson Reagan
(1911-)
40th President

Term—1981 to 1988

First Lady—Nancy Davis Reagan

Vice President—George Bush

Political Party—Democratic-turned-Republican

Home State—California

Career—actor, governor

Fun Facts

- Reagan is the first president to have been divorced.
- Reagan was the oldest person to become president at age 69.
- While he was a lifeguard, Reagan rescued 77 people.

Bookmark # 31-39

SECTION VII: IMPORTANT PEOPLE | 99

EXPLORERS

Admiral Richard Byrd
(1888–1957)

- On May 9, 1926, Richard Byrd of Virginia raised money to complete an airplane trip across the North Pole. Some people still doubt that he was successful.
- Byrd also made the dangerous trip over the South Pole in November 1929.
- Byrd mapped much of the coast of the Antarctic in his explorations during 1933-1934 and 1931-1941. His base near Ross Sea was called "Little America."

Bookmark # 32-2

EXPLORERS

Christopher Columbus
(1451–1506)

- In 1476, Columbus was on a ship that sunk after an attack. He had to swim six miles to the coast of Portugal.
- Columbus wasn't allowed to start his famous voyage until after sailors, ships, and supplies became available after Spain won the battles with the Moors.
- Crews on the *Nina*, *Pinta*, and *Santa Maria* talked of mutiny during the 1492 voyage, but there has been little evidence of true mutiny.

Bookmark # 32-3

EXPLORERS

Hernando Cortés
(1485–1547)

Hernando Cortés of Spain traveled to Mexico with hopes of finding riches. At first, Montezuma, the Aztec chief, didn't know if the white men who arrived were enemies or gods, and sent many expensive gifts. Cortés accepted the gifts, but fought the Aztecs anyway. The fight was easy when the Aztecs fled in fear because they had never seen horses, and thought a horse and rider were one being.

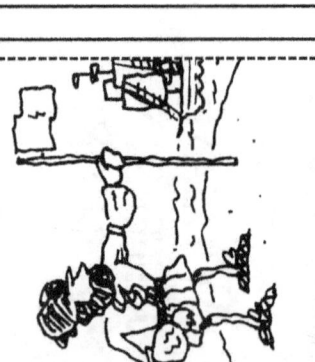

Bookmark # 32-4

EXPLORERS

Jacques Cousteau
(1910–1997)

- In addition to Jacques Cousteau's famous explorations of the ocean's depths, he improved the quality of the aqualung and built a camera that could take pictures 600 feet below the surface of the sea.
- In 1963, Cousteau and four other men spent an entire month living 33 feet below the Red Sea off the coast of Egypt.
- The television show *The Undersea World of Jacques Cousteau* ran four times a year from 1968-1975.

Bookmark # 32-5

EXPLORERS

Sir Edmund Hillary
(1919–)

- About 11:30 A.M. on May 29, 1953, Sir Edmund Hillary of New Zealand became the first known person to reach the peak of Mount Everest, at 29,028 feet.
- Hillary's expedition was led by Colonel John Hunt. His Sherpa guide, Tensing Norgay, also reached the summit during that expedition.
- The expedition battled up to 100-mile-per-hour winds, freezing temperatures, and other weather hazards. The air was so thin that the men had to carry oxygen tanks as part of the many supplies.

Bookmark # 32-6

EXPLORERS

Hernando de Soto (1496?-1542)

- De Soto's family wanted him to be a lawyer, but he was determined to be a conquistador instead.
- In 1539, de Soto led an expedition to conquer La Florida. Native Americans kept telling him of riches farther northeast. Two years later, de Soto and his party became the first Europeans to see the Mississippi River.
- When de Soto died, his men weighted his body with stones and sank him in a river so that Native Americans would not find out about his death.

Bookmark # 32-11

EXPLORERS

Juan Ponce de León (1460-1521)

- According to legend, anyone who drinks from the Fountain of Youth will live forever.
- Ponce de León set out to find the Fountain of Youth on March 3, 1513. A month later, he landed on the coast of Florida near what is now St. Augustine.
- At age 61, Ponce de León was still searching for the Fountain of Youth when a Native American fatally wounded him with an arrow.

Bookmark # 32-10

EXPLORERS

Marco Polo (1254-1324)

- At age 17, Marco Polo of Venice joined his father and uncle on an extended journey through much of the known world.
- While on the journey, Polo became an agent of Kublai Khan of China and was able to continue his travels.
- Polo was imprisoned after battling Genoa. A fellow prisoner named Rustichello wrote the stories Polo told him in a book called *The Description of the World*. Columbus took the book on his 1492 voyage.

Bookmark # 32-9

EXPLORERS

Francisco Pizarro (1482-1541)

Francisco Pizarro of Italy was with Balboa when he discovered the Pacific Ocean. In 1532, Pizarro set out to conquer the Incan empire of South America. He captured the Incan chief Atahualpa and asked for a ransom of a room filled with gold and two chambers filled with silver. Atahualpa's followers agreed. Pizarro's group melted the priceless artifacts into bars. Pizarro ordered that Atahualpa be killed by strangulation, then took over the empire himself.

Bookmark # 32-8

EXPLORERS

Ferdinand Magellan (1888-1957)

On September 20, 1519, Ferdinand Magellan of Portugal took 250 sailors and five ships to search for a western passage to the Indies through South America. By the time he rounded the southern tip of South America, one ship had been wrecked and another ship had returned to Spain. Magellan was killed when he was ambushed by warriors in the Philippines. Only 18 of the original 250 crew members were able to return to Spain about three years after the journey began. That ship, *Victoria*, was the first to sail around the world.

Bookmark # 32-7

SECTION VII: IMPORTANT PEOPLE | 101

IMPORTANT PE★PLE
Susan B. Anthony
(1820-1906)

- Teacher Susan B. Anthony was frustrated at being paid less than male teachers for doing the same work and for women being denied the right to vote. She started working for women's rights.

- Anthony and 15 other women voted in the national election on November 5, 1872, even though it was illegal for women to vote at the time. They were arrested two weeks later. Anthony never paid her fine of $100.

- The 19th Amendment gave women the right to vote exactly 100 years after Anthony's birth.

Bookmark # 33-1

IMPORTANT PE★PLE
Benedict Arnold
(1741-1801)

- Although George Washington greatly admired him, Arnold was known for risking lives foolishly and going against the rules of the military.

- After Arnold married Peggy Shippen, who was loyal to the British, he started to help the British.

- After Americans discovered Arnold's betrayal, he fled to London to escape punishment.

Bookmark # 33-2

IMPORTANT PE★PLE
Daniel Boone
(1734-1820)

- As a boy, Daniel Boone learned how to survive in the wilderness from the Delaware Indians who lived near his family.

- Boone's daughter and two other girls were once kidnapped by Shawnee Indians. Boone spent two days tracking them and rescued the girls.

- In 1915, Daniel Boone was elected to the Hall of Fame for Great Americans.

Bookmark # 33-3

IMPORTANT PE★PLE
George Washington Carver
(1860-1943)

- George Washington Carver was born a slave in Diamond Grove, Missouri. When he was an infant, he and his mother were captured by Confederate slave raiders. Carver was ransomed in exchange for a racehorse and was raised by relatives.

- Carver is famous for his experiments with plants, especially peanuts. He developed over 300 products from peanuts, such as shampoo, shaving cream, and linoleum.

- Carver once cooked an entire meal in which each menu item was made from peanuts. The guests ate soup, salad, creamed mock chicken, bread, candy, cake, ice cream, and coffee.

Bookmark # 33-4

IMPORTANT PE★PLE
"Buffalo Bill" Cody
(William Fredrick Cody)
(1846-1917)

- "Wild Bill" Hickok taught "Buffalo Bill" Cody about following a trail and defending himself without starting a fight.

- According to legend, when Cody was 12 years old, he shot a Native American to save the life of a white man. Cody was unhappy about the event because many of his friends were Native Americans.

- By the age of 14, Cody was a Pony Express rider. He once fooled a band of bandits by hiding money in his saddle blanket and giving them a pouch full of blank paper.

Bookmark # 33-5

102 | BOOKMARKS ACROSS THE CURRICULUM

IMPORTANT PE★PLE
Sam Houston
(1793-1863)

- Sam Houston wanted to make the army his career until he was reprimanded for dressing like the Cherokee Indians.
- After fighting at the Battle of San Jacinto and injuring his ankle, Houston was elected the first president of the Texas Republic.

Bookmark # 33-10

IMPORTANT PE★PLE
Nathan Hale
(1755-1776)

Nathan Hale strongly believed in American independence from Britain. He became a spy, and made sketches and diagrams of what he saw behind enemy lines to help the cause of the Revolutionary War. The British didn't think a teacher would help the military, but they discovered Hale's secret while he was on a spy mission to Long Island. The British offered him the opportunity to become a double spy instead of death, but Hale said, "I only regret that I have but one life to lose for my country." He was hanged on September 22, 1776.

Bookmark # 33-9

IMPORTANT PE★PLE
Benjamin Franklin
(1706-1790)

- Ben Franklin's curiosity led him to new inventions and discoveries. His most famous experiment with a kite and a key proved that lightning is electricity.
- Some of Franklin's inventions include bifocal eyeglasses, the Franklin stove, and the lightning rod.
- Franklin wrote *Poor Richard's Almanac*, filled with weather information, poems, calendars, recipes, and fun sayings such as "A penny saved is a penny earned" and "Fish and visitors stink in three days."

Bookmark # 33-8

IMPORTANT PE★PLE
Thomas Edison
(1847-1931)

- After three months of school, Edison's teacher called him "addlebrained." Edison's mother began teaching him at home.
- When he was 12, Edison sold newspapers, candy, vegetables, and fruit on a train that ran between Port Huron and Detroit. He set up a laboratory on the train and was fired when a chemical fell to the floor and burst into flames.

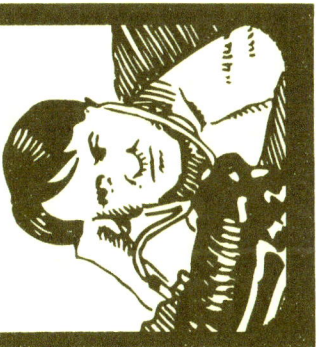

Bookmark # 33-7

IMPORTANT PE★PLE
Crazy Horse
(1845?-1887)

- When Crazy Horse was a boy in the Oglala tribe, his name was "Tashunca-uitco," which may mean "Curly." He took his father's name of Crazy Horse when he became a man.
- To save their land, Crazy Horse led 3,000 Native Americans on an attack of General George Armstrong Custer's troops at Little Big Horn in 1875. Custer and more than 200 of his followers died in that battle.
- Jealous Native Americans told white soldiers that Crazy Horse planned to lead a revolt. The solders arrested and stabbed Crazy Horse, who died the following day.

Bookmark # 33-6

SECTION VII: IMPORTANT PEOPLE | 103

IMPORTANT PEOPLE
Robert E. Lee
(1807-1870)

- Robert E. Lee grew up listening to his father tell stories of fighting beside George Washington during the Revolutionary War.
- President Lincoln offered Lee a chance to command the Union Army, but Lee decided to be loyal to his home state of Virginia.
- Lee was known for his good nature and kind, courteous ways. He even called the enemy "those people" or "our friends across the river."

Bookmark # 33-11

IMPORTANT PEOPLE
Horace Mann
(1796-1859)

- Horace Mann is known for his efforts to abolish slavery, improve treatment of the insane, and especially improve education. His motto was "Teach the people."
- To be able to afford books for school, Mann braided straw for a small factory that made straw hats and bonnets.

"Teach the people."

Bookmark # 33-12

IMPORTANT PEOPLE
Ivan Pavlov
(1849-1936)

Russian psychologist Ivan Pavlov experimented with dogs and what he called their "conditioned reflex" to help explain how learning takes place. He found that if a bell rang each time a dog was fed, the dog would eventually salivate when it heard the sound of a bell even if no food was visible. In 1904, Pavlov received the Nobel Prize for his work.

Bookmark # 33-13

IMPORTANT PEOPLE
Paul Revere
(1735-1818)

- When he was 13, Revere became an apprentice silversmith at his father's shop. He later opened his own silver business.
- Revere was one of the leaders of the Revolution. He took part in the Boston Tea Party.
- On April 18, 1775, Revere arranged for two lanterns to be placed in the steeple of the Old North Church as a signal that the British were about to invade by sea.

Bookmark # 33-14

IMPORTANT PEOPLE
Sally Ride
(1951-)

- Sally Ride didn't think about becoming an astronaut as a child because there weren't any astronauts at the time!
- At one time, the kids that Ride was babysitting told her that she had put the peanut butter and jelly in the wrong order on the sandwiches. She made new ones.
- Tennis star Billie Jean King thought Ride could have been a professional tennis player.
- On June 18, 1983, Ride became the first woman and the youngest American astronaut to circle Earth in a spacecraft during the second flight of *Challenger*.

Bookmark # 33-15

104 | BOOKMARKS ACROSS THE CURRICULUM

Bookmark # 33-16

IMPORTANT PE★PLE

Sacajawea
(1786?-1884)

- Charbonneau, Sacajawea, and their baby joined the Lewis and Clark Expedition. Sacajawea helped bargain for horses and other supplies. Once when the boat tipped, she rescued many of the items that fell overboard.
- Lewis and Clark paid Charbonneau for his work, but didn't pay Sacajawea.

Bookmark # 33-17

IMPORTANT PE★PLE

Deborah Sampson
(1759 or 1760-1827)

- As a child, Deborah Sampson learned how to do all the chores the boys did.
- Sampson disguised herself as a man named "Robert Shurtliff" and joined the Continental Army on May 20, 1782.
- After she was injured, a doctor discovered Deborah's secret. He encouraged her to tell her superior officers. She did.
- Private Robert Shurtliff was honorably discharged in October 1783. "He" was commended for bravery and good conduct.

Bookmark # 33-18

IMPORTANT PE★PLE

Sojourner Truth
(1797?-1883)

- The name given to Sojourner Truth at her birth about 1797 was Isabelle Van Wagener. At the age of nine, she was sold as a slave for a price of $50 and 100 sheep.
- Isabelle's owner set her free in 1827. In 1843, she changed her name and traveled to give speeches about God, against slavery, and for women's rights.
- Abraham Lincoln invited Truth to the White House in 1864 to recognize her for her efforts in gathering supplies for the Union Army.

Bookmark # 33-19

IMPORTANT PE★PLE

King Tut
(1370 B.C.?-1352 B.C.)

- Because the pharaoh Tutankhamen, or "King Tut," became king at age 9, he had the nickname "The Boy King."
- King Tut died at the age of 18 or 19.
- British archeologist Howard Carter found the tomb of King Tut in November 1922. Although Tut wasn't a major pharaoh, the discovery was a major find because the tomb had not yet been robbed of the nearly 2,000 objects buried with him. Researchers were able to learn a great deal of history from the tomb.

SECTION VII: IMPORTANT PEOPLE | 105

Section VIII

Daily Life

LANGUAGES & CODES

Foreign Terms

Hello
- French—*hol`* or *allô* (on the phone)
- German—*hallo*
- Italian—*pronto* or *pronti* (on the phone)
- Spanish—*hola*

Good-bye
- French—*adieu*
- German—*auf wiedersehen* or *lebewohl*
- Italian—*addio* or *arrivederci*
- Spanish—*adiós* or *hasta luego*

Friend
- French—*ami* (male) or *amie* (female)
- German—*freund*
- Italian—*amico* (male) or *amica* (female)
- Spanish—*amigo* or *amiga*

Bookmark # 34-3

LANGUAGES & CODES

Braille

- Louis Braille was blinded at the age of three. He grew up to invent the system of six raised dots that lets blind people read and write by running their fingertips over the paper.
- The Braille system is based on a system the military used for soldiers to be able to read and write in the dark.
- A special typewriter is used to form the Braille symbols. Braille includes not only letters of the alphabet, but also punctuation, symbols, such as math signs, and abbreviations.

a b c
d e f

Bookmark # 34-2

LANGUAGES & CODES

American Sign Language

- American Sign Language, which uses gestures to indicate words, allows people who are deaf or hearing impaired to communicate without speaking or writing.
- Laurent Clerc and Thomas Hopkins Gallaudet established America's first permanent school for people who are deaf in Hartford, Connecticut. American Sign Language was developed at that school.
- American Sign Language is based on a language children from that school used, with elements of the French Sign Language added later.

Bookmark # 34-1

LANGUAGES & CODES

More Foreign Terms

Please
- French—*s'il vous plaît*
- German—*gefallen* or *angenehm sein*
- Italian—*per favore* or *prego* or *per placere*
- Spanish—*por favor*

Thank you
- French—*grâce*
- German—*danke*
- Italian—*grazie*
- Spanish—*gracias*

Yes
- French—*oui* or *si*
- German—*ja* or *jawohl*
- Italian—*si* or *già*
- Spanish—*si*

No
- French—*non* or *pas*
- German—*nein*
- Italian—*no* or *non* or *punto* or *mica*
- Spanish—*no*

Bookmark # 34-4

LANGUAGES & CODES

Morse Code

- Samuel Morse filed for a patent for the Morse code in 1844. The patent was granted in 1849.
- Morse code, used primarily for transmitting information by telegraph, uses dots and dashes to represent each letter of the alphabet. The code can also be used with a light source such as a flashlight.
- The high classes of Ham Radio licenses require knowledge of the Morse code to communicate in the high-frequency bands.

Morse — — · — — · /

Code · — — · · · — ·

Bookmark # 34-5

LANGUAGES & CODES

Semaphore

- Semaphore is the method of signaling with flags in different positions to send messages. The flags are usually square and divided diagonally, with the upper part a solid red and the lower part a solid yellow.
- Lights instead of flags are sometimes used in semaphore.
- The semaphore code was invented in the 1700s to help ships communicate with each other at sea.
- Semaphore is rarely used today because radio and telephone communication is much easier.

Bookmark # 34-6

RELIGION

BUDDHISM

- Prince Siddhartha Gautama of India founded the Buddhism religion about 2,500 years ago. He was known as Buddha, which means "Enlightened One" in the Sanskrit language.
- The primary Buddhist writings are contained in a number of sacred books called the *Pali Canon*.
- The largest populations of people who follow Buddhism live in Southeast Asia.

Bookmark # 35-1

RELIGION

CHRISTIANITY

- Christianity began about 2,000 years ago with the birth of Jesus Christ.
- The writings of Christianity are contained in the *Holy Bible*, of which many translations and modern language editions are available. Many of these editions are based on the King James Version.
- Some other religions, such as Mormon, also use the King James Version of the Bible with additional books.
- Christianity includes Roman Catholic, Protestants of all types, and members of the Eastern Orthodox Church.

Bookmark # 35-2

---

108 | BOOKMARKS ACROSS THE CURRICULUM

RELIGION
CONFUCIANISM

- The philosopher K'ung Fu-tzu founded Confucianism about 2,500 years ago. His name, meaning "The Master Kung," is known in Latin as Confucius.

- The teachings of Confucianism are contained in *The Analects*, named for the Greek word *analekta*, meaning "a collection of facts and sayings." Some Chinese fortune cookie messages contain the teachings of Confucius.

- Most followers of Confucianism live in China and Taiwan.

Bookmark # 35-3

RELIGION
HINDUISM

- Hinduism is the European name for the *Sanatana Dharma*, which means "The Eternal Law."

- The earliest text for the Hindu religion is the *Rig Veda*, which dates back at least 3,000 years. The most popular text is the *Bhagavad Gita*, which teaches the art of yoga.

- One of the most well-known beliefs of the Hindu religion is that the cow is sacred.

- Most of the followers of Hinduism live in India and in communities established by the people of India.

Bookmark # 35-4

RELIGION
ISLAM

- The prophet Mohammed, who lived from 570 to 632, founded the Islam religion about 1,400 years ago. Mohammed was known for his extreme kindness. According to legend, he once cut off his sleeve so that he would not disturb the cat sleeping on it.

- Arab scholars wrote the teachings of Islam in the *Koran* about 20 years after Mohammed died because he was unable to read or write.

- Followers of Islam are known as Moslems or Muslims.

Bookmark # 35-5

RELIGION
JUDAISM

- The Hebrew chieftain Abraham founded the Judaism religion about 4,000 years ago. Abraham taught people to worship one God, known as Jehovah or Yahweh.

- The primary teachings of Judaism are contained in the *Torah* and the *Talmud*. Many teachings of Judaism follow the Old Testament.

- Judaism is now divided into Orthodox, Conservative, and Reformed groups.

- People who follow Judaism teachings are located throughout the world, with large populations in the United States, Israel, Europe, and Russia.

Bookmark # 35-6

RELIGION
SHINTO

- Shinto is a Japanese folk religion. Jimmu Tenno, the emperor of Japan in the early sixth century, is regarded as having unified the Japanese descendants of the Sun Goddess Amaterasu O-mikami.

- No holy book specific to Shinto was written. Many of the teachings of Shinto are derived from Confucianism and Buddhism.

- The main feature of Shinto is worship of both national heroes and family ancestors.

- Shinto was Japan's state religion from 1867 to 1945. In 1946, Emperor Hirohito, who became constitutional monarch, officially renounced Shinto.

Bookmark # 35-7

SECTION VIII: DAILY LIFE | 109

RELIGION
SIKHISM

- Guru Nanak of India founded the religion of Sikhism, developed from Hinduism, about 500 years ago. Guru Nanak, who lived from 1469 to 1539, was the first of 10 teachers of the Sikh followers.
- Guru Arjun compiled the main writings of Sikhism in 1604. The collection is known as *Adi Granth*, a Punjabi phrase meaning "The Original (or First) Book."
- The five main rules of life are the "5 Ks": *kes* (not trimming the hair or beard), *kacch* (knee-length trousers), *kara* (iron bangle), *kirpan* (sword), and *khanga* (comb).

Bookmark # 35-8

RELIGION
TAOISM

- The religion of Taoism was founded in prehistoric times. The earliest recorded mention of Taoism was by philosopher Lao-tzu, who lived about 570-490 B.C.
- Tao is the Chinese word for "path" or "way" and refers to the path of contentment and withdrawal. Taoists believe that path should be chosen over the path of self-serving and worldly ambition.
- The *Tao-Te Ching* is the religious work that contains the beliefs of and stories about Taoism.

Bookmark # 35-9

RELIGION
ZOROASTRIANISM

- Prophet Zoroaster (or Zarathustra) saw heavenly visions and founded the religion of Zoroastrianism in Persia (now Iran) about 3,000 years ago.
- The primary teachings of Zoroastrianism concern the war between Ormazd (good) and Ahriman (evil). The writings are found in *Gathas*, meaning "hymns," written in Avestan, a language similar to Sanskrit.

Bookmark # 35-10

MYTHS & FOLKLORE
MYTHS

- A myth is a story or legend that is passed on from generation to generation.
- Myths often tell the story of how something in nature, such as a rainbow, began or why animals act the way they do, such as a cat washing itself.
- Characters in myths often have supernatural or other fantastic powers.

Bookmark # 36-1

MYTHS & FOLKLORE
FOLKLORE

- Folklore is the beliefs, stories, dances, songs, and other customs passed down from generation to generation. Much of folklore is not written, but oral.
- In the early to mid-1800s, Jacob and Wilhelm Grimm of Germany collected folklore that included "Rapunzel," "Hansel and Gretel," "Rumpelstiltskin," and more than 200 other stories and tales.
- Hans Christian Andersen also collected and wrote many fairy tales and other stories, including "The Little Mermaid," "The Nightingale," and about 150 more.

Bookmark # 36-2

MYTHS & FOLKLORE
Some Greek Gods

- Ares—god of war
- Dionysus or Lycaeus—god of wine and merriment
- Eros—god of love
- Helios—god of the Sun
- Hercules—god of strength (son of Zeus, actually a hero, not a god)
- Hermes or Psychopompus—god of commerce; messenger of Zeus
- Hypnos—god of sleep
- Morpheus—god of dreams
- Pan—god of sheep
- Phoebus Apollo—god of sun, truth, music, healing
- Poseidon—ruler of the sea
- Zeus—god of thunder; ruler of the sky

Bookmark # 36-3

MYTHS & FOLKLORE
Some Greek Goddesses

- Aphrodite or Anadyomena—goddess of love and beauty
- Artemis, Orthia, or Phoebe—goddess of wild things
- Eos—goddess of the dawn
- Hera—goddess of marriage
- Hestia—goddess of the home
- Iris—goddess of the rainbow
- Maia—goddess of the fields (eldest of the seven Pleides, lover of Zeus, but not a goddess)
- Nike—goddess of victory
- Pallas Athena—goddess of the city, education, science, and war

Bookmark # 36-4

MYTHS & FOLKLORE
Some Roman Gods

- Amor or Cupid—god of love
- Apollo—god of sun, truth, music, and healing
- Janus—god of good beginnings
- Jupiter or Jove—god of thunder; ruler of the sky
- Mars—god of war
- Mercury—god of speed; a messenger
- Neptune—ruler of the sea
- Pluto—god of the Underworld
- Saturn—protector of planters
- Sol—god of the sun
- Somnus—god of sleep
- Vulcan or Mulciber—god of the fire or forge

Bookmark # 36-5

MYTHS & FOLKLORE
Some Roman Goddesses

- Aurora or Mater Matuta—goddess of the dawn
- Diana—goddess of the hunt
- Fauna—goddess of the fields
- Flora—goddess of flowers
- Fortuna—goddess of chance and good luck
- Juno—goddess of marriage
- Luna—goddess of the moon
- Minerva—goddess of the city, education, science, and war
- Venus—goddess of love and beauty
- Vesta—goddess of the home
- Victoria—goddess of victory

Bookmark # 36-6

MYTHS & FOLKLORE
Atlantis

- About 370 B.C., Plato wrote of Poseidon, god of the sea, whose son Triton ruled Atlantis, a city or even whole continent once located in the Atlantic Ocean.
- Some people believe Atlantis actually existed at one time, while others think the place is a myth. Some people have spent thousands of dollars searching for Atlantis.
- The civilization of Atlantis was greatly advanced for its time.
- According to legend, the gods destroyed the city when the leaders became too egotistical and the people became too self-satisfied.

Bookmark # 36-7

SECTION VIII: DAILY LIFE

MYTHS & FOLKLORE
BERMUDA TRIANGLE

- The Bermuda Triangle is located in the Atlantic Ocean in an area between Bermuda, Puerto Rico, and the southeast coast of Florida. The area is about 440,000 square miles in size.
- The legend of the Bermuda Triangle states that a high number of ships or airplanes—or just their crewmembers—disappear when crossing the Triangle.

Bookmark # 36-8

MYTHS & FOLKLORE
BIGFOOT

- The first report of an ape-like creature with big feet that measure well over 16 inches in length was made in 1811. Sightings of Bigfoot, also known as Sasquatch and other names, are concentrated in the northwestern United States.
- A creature similar to Bigfoot and called a Yeti or Abominable Snowman has been reported in Tibet.

Bookmark # 36-9

MYTHS & FOLKLORE
DOWSING

- Dowsing is a method some people believe will find water, gold, oil, or other valuable resource.
- Often, a "dowsing rod" in the shape of a Y is held with the point in front and each of the dowser's hands on one branch of the Y. The dowsing rod will bend down when the resource sought appears below the ground's surface.
- Some dowsers like to use a willow branch, but others use a different type of wood, a bent coat hanger, or other items. Some dowsers don't use a dowsing rod at all.

Bookmark # 36-10

MYTHS & FOLKLORE
DREAMS

According to superstition, someone who dreams about

- going up stairs or hills will have good fortune, but going down foretells bad luck.
- reading or studying books will have good luck.
- being in a tent will have a major change in his or her life.
- a crying baby will suffer disappointment.
- holidays will soon entertain interesting strangers.

Bookmark # 36-11

MYTHS & FOLKLORE
LOCH NESS MONSTER

- Reports of a strange animal in Loch Ness (a "loch" is a lake) of Scotland began in April 1933.
- More than 10,000 reports of sightings have been made.
- Some people believe the "monster" is actually a reptile similar to a dinosaur called a plesiosaur.
- Many of the photographs of the huge monster nicknamed "Nessie" have been proven to be fakes, but others cannot be proven or disproven.
- A Loch Ness Investigation Bureau has been established to investigate Nessie.

Bookmark # 36-12

112 | BOOKMARKS ACROSS THE CURRICULUM

MYTHS & FOLKLORE
MEDUSA

The Medusa was a female monster from Greek mythology that had snakes growing out of her head like hair. Anyone who looked into her face would turn to stone. To defeat her, the Greek hero Perseus chopped off her head. Instead of looking directly at her, he looked only at her reflection in his shiny shield.

Bookmark # 36-13

MYTHS & FOLKLORE
PHRENOLOGY

- Phrenology is an unproved method of examining bumps on the skull in at least 35 different places to determine intelligence and character traits.
- The location and size of the bumps are said to tell how honest, kind, and hardworking someone is.
- Phrenology began in the 1790s and was at the peak of popularity in the 1830s and 1840s.
- People hired phrenologists to help them decide whom to hire for jobs, whom to marry, what careers they should pursue, and more.

Bookmark # 36-14

MYTHS & FOLKLORE
PREMONITIONS

A premonition is a feeling or vision of something that will happen in the future. President Abraham Lincoln dreamed he saw people crying as he walked through the White House. When he saw a coffin, he asked someone who had died. The man in his dream told him the president had been assassinated. Lincoln was assassinated soon after having this dream.

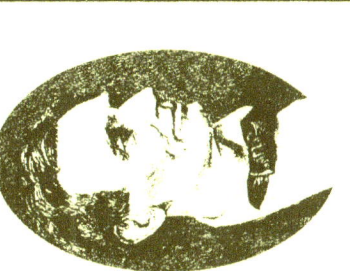

Bookmark # 36-15

MYTHS & FOLKLORE
SUPERSTITIONS

A superstition is a belief with no proof of its truth. Some superstitions include

- A black cat crossing someone's path is bad luck, but a black cat walking toward a person is lucky.
- Feeding strange pigeons brings new friends.
- Anyone who picks dandelions will wet the bed.
- Rubbing an apple before eating it brings good luck.
- Someone's left palm itching for no apparent reason means the person will get money. If the person's right palm itches, he or she will meet someone important.

Bookmark # 36-16

MYTHS & FOLKLORE
UNICORNS

- Unicorns are usually described as white horses with long flowing manes and tails. The mythical beasts are known mostly for the single horn growing out of their foreheads. The horns supposedly had magical properties used to detect poisons and to prevent and cure various diseases.
- Some say the unicorns are extinct because they either missed the ark or were all killed for their horns.

Bookmark # 36-17

SECTION VIII: DAILY LIFE

MYTHS & FOLKLORE

Unidentified Flying Objects

- Many people think beings from other planets visit Earth in flying saucers or Unidentified Flying Objects (UFOs).
- In 1938, actor Orson Welles broadcast a radio show of author H. G. Wells's fiction work *War of the Worlds*. The radio show included "news bulletins" that told of Martians attacking New Jersey. Many people thought the show was a news broadcast and believed Martians actually were landing.
- Some people say that Ezekiel in the Bible actually saw a UFO when he saw a wheel within a wheel.

Bookmark # 36-18

CLOTHING & FASHION

Beards

- Ancient Egyptians wouldn't grow beards because having a beard was against their religion.
- Alexander the Great made his soldiers stay clean-shaven so that the enemy couldn't grab them by their beards.
- The Romans used to let their beards grow during times of mourning, while the Greeks shaved during times of mourning.

Bookmark # 37-1

CLOTHING & FASHION

Shoes

- Fashion during the 14th century called for long, pointed shoes. The points were up to 20 inches beyond the big toe. The points were stuffed with moss to help them keep their shape. The Church considered these shoes to be the work of the devil.
- Early in the 16th century, shoes were so wide that King Henry VIII decreed that no shoe could be wider than 6 inches.
- High heels were first worn in the late 16th century. At the time, both women and men wore heels.

Bookmark # 37-2

CLOTHING & FASHION

Tattoos

- Getting a tattoo is painful and can be dangerous.
- The ink in many tattoos is black, but the yellowish or brownish color of the skin of most Caucasians makes the color appear to be blue.
- Tattooing used to be done for religious reasons or to show to which group someone belonged. Sailors often had anchors tattooed on their forearms.
- Some African tribes once had a custom of tattooing the tongue to show grief.

Bookmark # 37-3

CLOTHING & FASHION

Umbrellas

- The first umbrellas were likely large leaves held over the head.
- The umbrella, also called a "bumbershoot" or "parasol," was invented before anyone learned to write.
- The word *umbrella* comes from the Latin word *umbra*, meaning "shade."
- For thousands of years, umbrellas were used only for protection from the sun. Umbrellas have been used for protection from the rain for only about 300 years.
- One job of ancient slaves was to hold umbrellas for their owners.

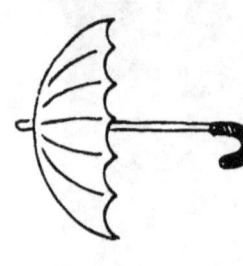

Bookmark # 37-4

114 | BOOKMARKS ACROSS THE CURRICULUM

CLOTHING & FASHION
Underwear

- King Tut had 145 pairs of linen loincloths (underwear) buried with him in his tomb in 1352 B.C.
- During the Middle Ages, men's underwear had strings around the waist to keep them from falling down.
- At one time people used underwear mostly as a way to keep the dirt from their unwashed skin from getting on their fancy outer clothing.
- Some other names for men's underwear include boxer shorts (or boxers), breechcloths, briefs, drawers, long johns, skivvies, and union suits.

Bookmark # 37-5

FOODS
Chocolate

- In 1519, the Aztec chief Montezuma offered the invader Hernando Cortés *xocolatl* (chocolate) to drink.
- Cocoa beans from Central America were taken to Spain in 1521. The recipe for preparing drinking chocolate from cocoa, sugar, vanilla, and cinnamon was a state secret.
- At first, chocolate was made with water instead of milk, and people drank chocolate without sugar. Instead, they flavored the chocolate with spices.

Bookmark # 38-1

FOODS
Ice Cream

- Ice cream is thought to have been invented in China about 2000 B.C. It was eaten in Italy in the 17th century, and came to America in the early 18th century.
- The first ice cream factory opened in Baltimore, Maryland, in 1851.
- The first ice cream sundae was made in E. C. Berner's ice cream parlor in Two Rivers, Wisconsin, about 1890. A customer suggested Berner pour chocolate syrup over a scoop of ice cream in a dish. The treat was originally sold only on Sundays, which is how it got its name. "Blue Laws" forbade selling soda water for ice cream sodas on Sunday, so the "sundae" was invented.
- The first ice cream cone possibly was made in New Jersey in 1896. Before this, ice cream was served in blocks. Another source says the cone originated at the St. Louis World's Fair in 1904.

Bookmark # 38-2

FOODS
Popcorn

Not all kinds of corn can be made into popcorn; the corn has to have the correct amount of water inside the kernel. Popcorn pops when the water inside the kernel expands with enough pressure that the hard starchy part of the kernel explodes. Microwaving popcorn improves the process because the kernel is heated from the inside out, resulting in a stronger explosion that makes larger, more tender kernels.

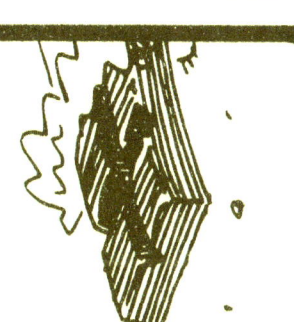

Bookmark # 38-3

FOODS
Pretzels

- According to legend, a monk in Italy invented pretzels about 1,500 years ago. He is said to have used pretzels as a reward for students who recited their religion studies correctly.
- Because people used to pray by crossing their arms across their chests, the shape of a pretzel is meant to look like the arms of a child in prayer. Pretzels now come in several shapes and flavors.
- A custom during the 17th century was that a bride and groom would pull apart a pretzel like a wishbone.

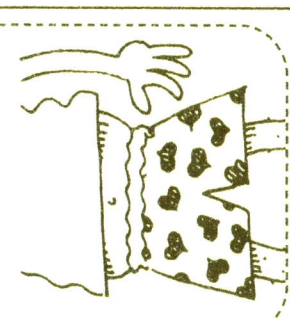

Bookmark # 38-4

SECTION VIII: DAILY LIFE | 115

FOODS — Salt

- The word *salary* is based on the custom of Roman soldiers receiving a *salarium* to buy salt rations.
- Slabs of salt have been used as money in the desert areas of Africa.
- Salt has at least 14,000 uses besides seasoning food. Some of its uses include tanning leather, preserving food, and as an ingredient in items such as soap and glass.
- In 1930, Mahatma Gandhi of India traveled to the sea to make salt as a protest against the salt tax.

Bookmark # 38-5

FOODS — Sandwiches

- Roman soldiers ate food similar to sandwiches over 2,000 years ago.
- Hamburgers get their name from the place they were invented: the port of Hamburg, Germany. Immigrants to America in the 1850s introduced hamburgers to America.
- American law says that hamburgers have to be made entirely of beef.

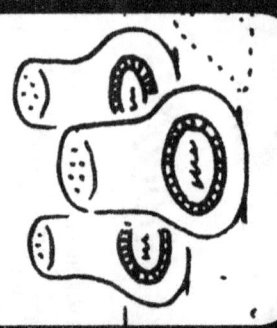

Bookmark # 38-6

FOODS — Spices

- Spices are made of various parts of plants, including the bark of trees, leaves, and seeds.
- Christopher Columbus discovered the New World while looking for a new route to the source of black pepper.
- Saffron, made from a tiny flower grown mostly in Spain, is the most expensive spice. About 250,000 flowers are needed to make one pound of spice.
- Zanzibar is sometimes called "The Isle of Cloves" because much of the world's supply of cloves comes from the island.

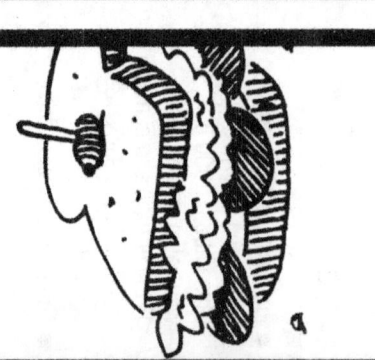

Bookmark # 38-7

FOODS — Miscellaneous Foods

- In 1573, potatoes were grown in Europe as ornamental plants. At the time, many people thought that potatoes were poisonous.
- The first patent for chewing gum in America was granted in 1871. The first bubble gum wasn't available in America until 1928.
- Garlic, now known to have some medicinal qualities, was once thought to prevent the plague, as well as scaring vampires.

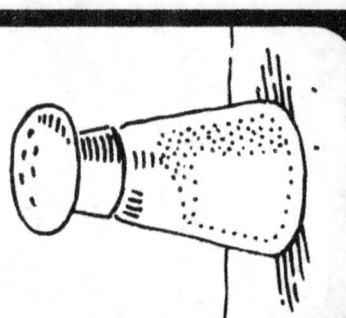

Bookmark # 38-8

Section IX

Inventions and Technology

COMPUTERS
Early Computers

- In 1852, Lady Augusta Ada Byron, Countess of Lovelace (1815-1852) of England became one of the first programmers on the "analytical engine," which was a simple computer. The computer language Ada is named for her.

- The first electronic computer was made at the University of Pennsylvania in 1946. The 30-ton machine, called the **E**lectronic **N**umerical **I**ntegrator and **C**alculator (ENIAC), was two stories high.

Bookmark # 39-1

COMPUTERS
Types of Computers

- mainframe—the largest and fastest of all computers; many people can use it at the same time
- servers—mini computers that have several processors and disk space
- personal computers—fit on a desk; first became available in 1971 when a TV screen was used for a monitor
- portable (notebook or laptop)—can be carried easily from place to place and is able to run on battery power
- personal digital assistant (PDA)—hand-held computer

Bookmark # 39-2

COMPUTERS
Main Computer Components

- CPU—contains the bulk of the computer memory and the central processing unit
- keyboard—the most common way to enter information into a computer
- modem—allows information to be transmitted over telephone lines
- mouse—a hand-operated device to enter information into the computer by the "point-and-click" method
- monitor—the screen to view data
- speakers—used to transmit sound quality from computer

Bookmark # 39-3

SECTION IX: INVENTIONS AND TECHNOLOGY | 117

COMPUTERS

Some Software

- databases—an electronic way of storing information
- games—used for entertainment or learning
- multimedia—used for sound or video
- operating systems—a series of programs that organize and control a computer
- spreadsheets—used to organize numbers or words into rows and columns
- utilities—used to keep the files on a computer organized
- word processing—used to type documents; often includes features such as spell-check

Bookmark # 39-4

COMPUTERS

Computer Languages

- Computer programs are written in a type of code called a computer language.
- For more than 2,000 different computer languages exist. Many of the languages are based on other languages with improvements or changes to make the new language compatible with a different computer operating system.
- A programmer must know algebra to be able to write in most computer languages.
- Some computer languages are Ada, ALGOL, Basic, C++, COBOL, Forth, Fortran, Java, LISP, Pascal, and PL/1.

Bookmark # 39-5

COMPUTERS

History of the Internet

- 1960s—the U.S. Department of Defense started a project to design a computer network with alternate routes in case of a nuclear attack
- 1970s—supercomputers across the country were linked to be able to share information
- 1980s—non-commercial information could be exchanged via a computer network
- 1990s—the network was opened up to everyone, including commercial companies and people with home computers; the Internet became a new way for people to communicate and shop

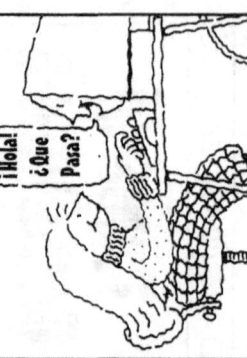

Bookmark # 39-6

COMPUTERS

Internet Address Abbreviations

- **ac**—an academic organization
- **co or com**—a for-profit company
- **edu**—an educational institution
- **gov**—a government organization
- **mil**—military
- **net**—an organization involved in running the Internet
- **org**—a non-profit organization

Bookmark # 39-7

COMPUTERS

E-Mail

- The term "e-mail" is short for "electronic mail," with which messages often can be sent quicker and more cheaply than regular mail, now nicknamed "snail mail."
- When someone sends an e-mail message, the computer sends it to a computer called a mail server. That server sends the message to another server, which sends the message to another server, and so on, until the message reaches its destination.
- The entire process of sending an e-mail message often takes less than a minute.

Bookmark # 39-8

TRANSPORTATION
Hot Air Balloons

- In 1783, Jean-Pierre Blanchard rode in a hot air balloon in France. When he hit turbulence over the English Channel, he threw everything he could overboard—including his pants.
- Ten years later, Blanchard demonstrated a hot air balloon in Philadelphia. President George Washington was there to watch the balloon take to the skies.

Bookmark # 40-5

TRANSPORTATION
Bicycles

- The first two-wheeler appeared in America in 1800. The "walk-along" had no gears or pedals.
- Pierre Lallement invented the "velocipede boneshaker" in the 1860s. The front wheel of these bicycles was much larger than the back wheel.
- The first official bicycle race took place in Hendon, England, in 1868.

Bookmark # 40-4

TRANSPORTATION
Automobiles' Working Parts

- The first wheels of cars were similar either to those of horse carts or bicycles. Wheels for horse carts were too heavy to function properly. Bicycle wheels were too weak and bent out-of-shape too easily.
- Early braking systems required a lot of muscle power from the driver.
- The basic systems of cars include brakes, electrical, exhaust, fuel, steering, and suspension.
- A small car has about 30,000 individual mechanical components.

Bookmark # 40-3

TRANSPORTATION
Early Automobiles

- In the mid-1700s, "horseless carriages" were powered by inconvenient steam engines. In 1860, Étienne Lenoir put an internal combustion engine between the wheels of an old horse cart.
- Many drivers of the unreliable early cars took horses along in case the car stalled.
- Early cars were a hazard, from mechanical problems to inexperienced drivers to the chaos created when the cars scared horses.
- Henry Ford of Detroit mass-produced his Model T Ford in 1908. The car was cheaper than a horse and buggy. Ford began assembly-line production in 1913.

Bookmark # 40-2

TRANSPORTATION
Airplanes

- Sir George Cayley invented the first successful glider in 1804. It had a kite-shaped wing mounted on a pole and a universally jointed tail unit.
- Wilbur and Orville Wright are credited with being the first to build a successful flying machine. Their first flight was December 17, 1903, near Kitty Hawk, North Carolina. The airplane stayed in the air for 59 seconds and traveled 260 meters (852 feet).

Bookmark # 40-1

SECTION IX: INVENTIONS AND TECHNOLOGY

TRANSPORTATION
Motorcycles

- The first motorcycle, built in 1885, had wooden wheels. Solid rubber wheels quickly replaced the wooden wheels. By 1888, air-filled tires were used to make the ride smoother.
- Some fast motorcycles carry a small container of nitrous oxide gas that's sprayed into the engine, producing extra power for a short time.
- Motorcycles can travel well over 242 miles per hour on a track with a long enough straight-away and a good surface.

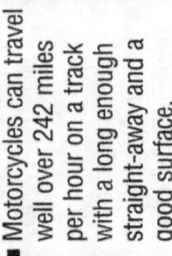

Bookmark # 40-6

TRANSPORTATION
Space Travel

- Escaping Earth's gravity requires a speed of 24,800 miles per hour.
- In July 1969, the Apollo Project saw men walk on the moon and return home safely. The astronauts were put in quarantine for 17 days in case they brought harmful germs back with them.
- When a capsule is in space, an error of one mile per hour in calculated speeds would make the capsule miss the moon by 1,000 miles.
- The first space shuttle, launched in 1981, was late returning to Earth by only a few seconds.

Bookmark # 40-7

TRANSPORTATION
Submarines

- The Ancient Greeks designed an underwater craft large enough for people. The "diving bell," as it was called because of its shape, couldn't move. The bell was suspended in the water by a rope.
- In 1620, Dutch inventor Cornelius Drebbel designed a submarine that could move. The submarine was made of wood covered in leather. Twelve men inside the sub moved it by rowing. That sub was able to stay underwater for 15 minutes and went 15 feet deep in the Thames River. King James I of Britain went on one of the test runs.

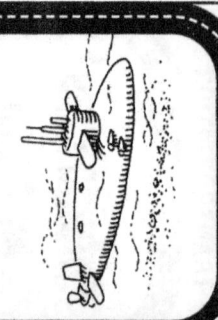

Bookmark # 40-8

TRANSPORTATION
Trains

- Horses pulled the first trains on wooden tracks in the 16th century.
- On February 21, 1804, Richard Trevithick's steam-powered train traveled nine and one-half miles in Wales. The trip took over two hours.
- Locomotives work equally well facing either forward or backward, saving workers from having to turn them around at the end of a line.
- The caboose used to be a place where workers could watch the train for possible problems, such as cars coming off the tracks. Now, electronics can detect problems.

Bookmark # 40-9

MISCELLANEOUS INVENTIONS
Bathtubs

- At one time, people used to bathe only in rivers, lakes, ponds, or other bodies of water. Finally, the Greeks and Romans built public bathhouses with hot and cold water. One Roman bathhouse could hold 3,200 bathers at the same time.
- The first bathtubs for individuals were so small that they were more like a sink. Eventually tubs became larger and larger.
- Bathtubs have been made from all types of materials, including wood, various metals, glass, porcelain, and more.

Bookmark # 41-1

120 | BOOKMARKS ACROSS THE CURRICULUM

MISCELLANEOUS INVENTIONS
Edison's Inventions

Thomas Edison invented over 1,000 items, including many improvements on others' ideas. His most famous invention is the phonograph, or gramophone, in 1877. Other inventions he improved upon or invented completely include the electric light bulb, a battery, an electric generator, motion picture film, telegraph, and telephone.

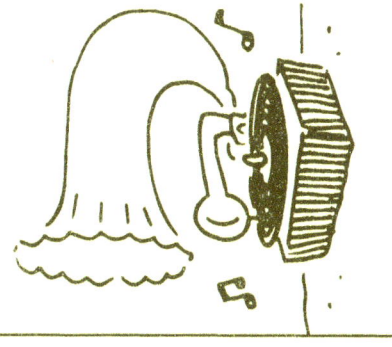

Bookmark # 41-6

MISCELLANEOUS INVENTIONS
Cotton Gin

Eli Whitney was asked to invent a machine that separated seed from the fiber of cotton. At the time, one person doing the task by hand would spend 10 hours to separate the lint or cotton fiber from three pounds of seeds. In one hour, Whitney's machine could do the same amount of work that took several people a week to complete. He received the patent for the cotton gin on March 14, 1794. The state of South Carolina gave him $50,000 in thanks.

Bookmark # 41-5

MISCELLANEOUS INVENTIONS
Cameras

- A camera is basically a box with a piece of light-sensitive film inside. The light enters the box through the lens, with the shutter controlling the amount of light.
- In 1827, the first successful photograph taken needed eight hours for exposure. In 1839, Louis Daguerre reduced the exposure time to a half-hour. Now exposure time is almost instantaneous.
- People in older photographs often aren't smiling because they had to pose so long for the photographer and holding a smile that long is difficult.

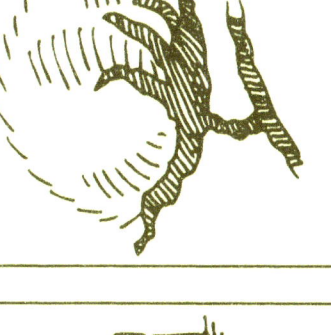

Bookmark # 41-4

MISCELLANEOUS INVENTIONS
Bridges

- An arch bridge curves upward with the ends pushing against a support.
- A beam bridge is built by laying beams of wood, steel, or concrete across an expanse.
- A cantilever bridge has beams that meet in the center and are anchored to the piers.
- A suspension bridge is hung from cables that are hung from towers on each side of the expanse.

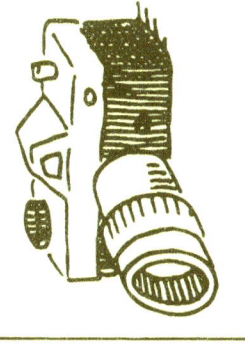

Bookmark # 41-3

MISCELLANEOUS INVENTIONS
Batteries

- As a rule, the larger the dry-cell battery, the longer it will last. AA batteries last longer than AAA batteries, and D batteries last longer than C batteries.
- The outside of batteries is often made of zinc to be used as a cathode (negative electrode).
- The carbon post in the center of the battery cell is an anode (positive electrode).
- The area between the outside of the battery and the center post is an electrolyte (a paste that conducts electric current).

Bookmark # 41-2

SECTION IX: INVENTIONS AND TECHNOLOGY

MISCELLANEOUS INVENTIONS

Glass

- Glass may have been invented by accident when some form of soda, sand, and limestone fell into a fire.
- The Egyptians built the first known glass factory about 1400 B.C.
- Tempered glass is made to be very strong and often nearly unbreakable. It is used in windows and other everyday objects. Bulletproof glass, used in places such as banks and taxicabs, is also a type of tempered glass.

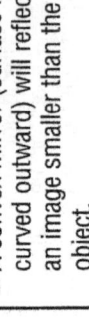

Bookmark # 41-7

MISCELLANEOUS INVENTIONS

Keys

- Locks were used by Egyptians as long as 4,000 years ago. The keys were often as much as two feet long.
- Most keys are made of metal—often brass, nickel, or aluminum. Sometimes wood or other material is used, but the keys don't last as long.
- Keys are used to lock many things, such as rooms or entire buildings, vehicles, desks, luggage, mailboxes, diaries, padlocks, and cabinets.

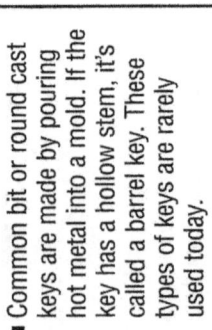

Bookmark # 41-8

MISCELLANEOUS INVENTIONS

Key Types

- Common bit or round cast keys are made by pouring hot metal into a mold. If the key has a hollow stem, it's called a barrel key. These types of keys are rarely used today.
- Stamped metal keys are cut from a large sheet of metal almost like the way some cookies are made. Virtually no difference appears between one key and another from the same sheet from which keys were stamped. Many luggage keys are made of stamped metal.
- Yale-type keys are specifically cut for accuracy and variety. Most keys are Yale-type keys.

Bookmark # 41-9

MISCELLANEOUS INVENTIONS

Matches

- In 1827, British pharmacist John Walker was trying to invent an explosive material for guns. He stirred the material with a stick and scraped the stick on the floor to remove the material. The material burst into a flame. He called the discovery a "congreve" after inventor Sir William Congreve.
- In 1836, Alonzo D. Philips received the first American patent on matches he called "locofocos."
- Matches used to be poisonous. Matches were used in many murders and suicides.

Bookmark # 41-10

MISCELLANEOUS INVENTIONS

Mirrors

- A flat mirror will reflect an image the same size as the object.
- A concave mirror (surface is curved inward) will reflect an image larger than the object. Some shiny concave surfaces, such as a spoon, reflect the image upside down.
- A convex mirror (surface is curved outward) will reflect an image smaller than the object.
- A two-way mirror acts as a regular mirror on one side and like a window on the other.
- Mirrors are often made of glass with a backing made of silver or mercury.

Bookmark # 41-11

MISCELLANEOUS INVENTIONS

Money

- The first coin was made in Lydia in Asia Minor about 650 B.C. The Chinese were the first to use paper money about A.D. 600.
- Some of the items that have been used for money include blankets, salt, shells, and soap.
- Franklin Delano Roosevelt is pictured on the dime in honor of his founding efforts for the March of Dimes charity against birth defects. A dime has 118 ridges around the edge.

Bookmark # 41-12

MISCELLANEOUS INVENTIONS

Nails

- Boat nails are shaped like a peg.
- Box nails have a very thin shaft.
- Common nails have a flat head.
- Finishing nails have small heads made to be driven beneath the surface.
- Flooring nails are made for floors.
- Roofing nails have domed heads.
- Scaffold nails have a small ledge under the head.

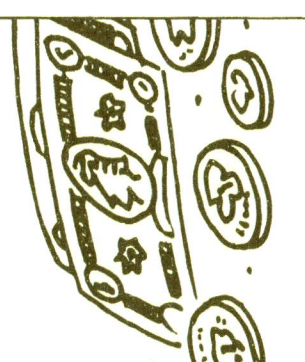

Bookmark # 41-13

MISCELLANEOUS INVENTIONS

Paper

- Most paper is made from wood, but paper can also be made from bamboo, cotton, grass, hemp, jute, linen, rags, straw, and other items with fibers. Recycled paper is made from other paper.
- The first paper was made from mulberry bark about 105 A.D. by Ts'ai Lun, a eunuch with the Eastern Han Court of the Chinese Emperor Ho Ti. Starting about 800 years ago, papyrus, a reed found along the Nile River in Egypt, was widely used for paper.
- Over 2,000 years ago, the Chinese were the first to use paper similar to the paper of today, but Europeans didn't use that type of paper until about 800 years ago.
- Natural paper is usually brown and has to be bleached white.

Bookmark # 41-14

MISCELLANEOUS INVENTIONS

Pencils

- The "lead" in pencils is actually graphite.
- The first wooden pencils with graphite centers were made in France about 1790.
- The graphite in early pencils was a square shape instead of the round shape of today.
- The number on pencils refers to the hardness of the graphite. The higher the number, the harder the graphite and the lighter the mark. Number 2 pencils are the most common and are fairly soft. Some companies use a combination of letters and numbers to indicate softness or hardness of the graphite.
- The inconvenience of having to sharpen pencils led to the invention of mechanical pencils that are always sharp.

Bookmark # 41-15

MISCELLANEOUS INVENTIONS

Robots

- An android is a machine built to look or act like a human.
- An automaton is a machine that works on its own.
- A cyborg is part human, part robot.
- A droid is a robot built only to serve its master.
- A probot is a personal robot for home use.
- A robotrix is a female robot.

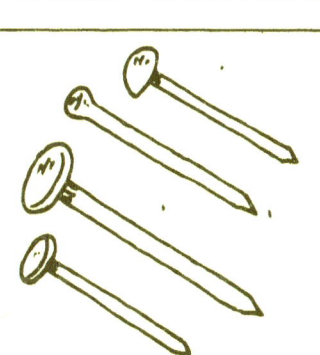

Bookmark # 41-16

SECTION IX: INVENTIONS AND TECHNOLOGY

MISCELLANEOUS INVENTIONS

Rockets

- Rockets range in size from small fireworks to the huge rockets launched into space.
- Military rockets were invented more than 2,000 years ago. Germans built the first of the modern rockets at the end of World War II.
- In 1947, an American rocket flew 669 miles per hour. Within 20 years, rockets were flying at 4,525 miles per hour within Earth's gravitational pull.
- In 1957, the Soviet Union's *Sputnik* traveled at a height of 550 miles and a speed of 17,000 miles per hour.

Bookmark # 41-17

MISCELLANEOUS INVENTIONS

Telephone

Bell Telephone asked Henry Dreyfuss to redesign the telephone in 1946 because the phones then were difficult to hold between the shoulder and the ear. He and his team spent 3,000 hours to make a sturdy phone that was more comfortable to use. The design chosen was described as "a lumpy rectangle." Dreyfuss hated that particular design. After a few minor changes to the original design, 161 million of the classic black desk phones were sold. The phone was nicknamed P.O.T.—for Plain Old Telephone.

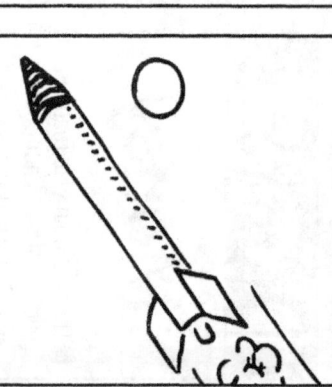

Bookmark # 41-18

MISCELLANEOUS INVENTIONS

Telescopes

- The smallest telescopes available now are more powerful than the one Galileo used in 1609.
- The telescope at Palomar weighs 29,000 pounds (14 tons). With that telescope, a scientist can see galaxies over two billion light-years away.
- Refractor telescopes consist of a series of lenses in a tube to transmit the image.
- Reflector telescopes use mirrors to transmit the image.
- Compound telescopes use a combination of refracting and reflecting means to transmit the image.

Bookmark # 41-19

MISCELLANEOUS INVENTIONS

Television

- The number of television sets in the United States increased from 10,000 to 60,000,000 between 1945 and 1960.
- The first TV commercial was for a Bulova clock on July 1, 1941.
- The first coast-to-coast television show broadcast in color was the Tournament of Roses parade at Pasadena, California, on January 1, 1954.

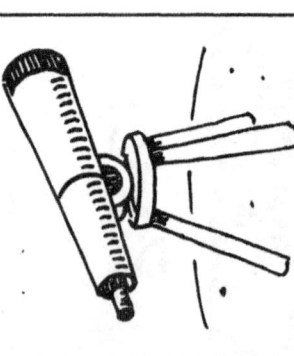

Bookmark # 41-20

MISCELLANEOUS INVENTIONS

Thermometer

- No one knows for certain who invented the first thermometer, but it has been attributed to Galileo. An astronomer from Florence, Italy, he made one of the first thermometers in 1593.
- One of the first types of thermometers had glass balls in tubes that rose and fell with the temperatures.
- Other types of thermometers now include dial, mercury (like those used in taking human temperatures), and digital.
- The tube in the type of mercury thermometer used to take people's temperature is only about the size of a human hair.

Bookmark # 41-21

124 | BOOKMARKS ACROSS THE CURRICULUM

MISCELLANEOUS INVENTIONS

Typewriter

- The first recorded attempt to make a typewriter-type instrument was by Henry Mill, a British inventor, in 1714.

- William Austin Burt, from America, made the first typewriter in 1829. That machine was made entirely of wood. At first, typing was slower than writing by hand. The letters on the keyboard were arranged as they are now to keep early typists from going too fast.

- The electric typewriter was first invented in the early 1900s, but wasn't widely used until the 1960s. Now, word processors have almost totally replaced typewriters.

- *Adventures of Huckleberry Finn* by Mark Twain was the first book known to have been written on a typewriter.

Bookmark # 41-23

MISCELLANEOUS INVENTIONS

Traffic Signals

- The first changeable traffic signal was installed in England in 1868. It had two "arms" to signal whether to stop or proceed. The signal was for pedestrians, not vehicles.

- In 1914, the first signal light using side-by-side red and green colors appeared in Cleveland, Ohio, to allow the signal to be seen at night. The three-way automatic signal light was invented by Garrett Morgan.

- The position of the lights was changed to up-and-down to help people who were color blind to distinguish the lights. Now, red lights have some orange color to them and green lights have blue in them, also to help those who are color blind.

Bookmark # 41-22

SECTION IX: INVENTIONS AND TECHNOLOGY | 125

Section X

Arts and Entertainment

MISCELLANEOUS ARTS: Holograms

- A hologram is a three-dimensional image created by a beam of laser light passing through a hologram wave interference photograph.
- At first, holograms were used primarily for wall decoration, magazine illustration, jewelry, keychains, and other items. Now, holograms are used to help make counterfeiting credit cards, driver's licenses, and other items more difficult.

Bookmark # 42-3

MISCELLANEOUS ARTS: Painters

- Leonardo da Vinci spent about three years painting the *Mona Lisa*.
- Michelangelo spent well over four years painting the ceiling of the Sistine Chapel in the early 1500s. He painted most of it lying on his back.
- Pablo Picasso finished more than 20,000 paintings in his life. He once finished 23 paintings in one month.
- Norman Rockwell used diapers for paint rags.

Bookmark # 42-2

MISCELLANEOUS ARTS: Types of Paintings

- Landscape paintings feature nature scenes.
- Seascape paintings feature ocean or sea scenes.
- Cityscape paintings feature city buildings.
- Portraits feature a person or persons.
- A still life painting features small objects, such as a bowl of fruit.
- Abstract paintings don't look exactly like anything in the real world.

Bookmark # 42-1

Section X: Arts and Entertainment | 127

MISCELLANEOUS ARTS
Sculpture

- A sculptor may shape a soft material, such as clay, or carve or chip away at a hard material, such as wood or marble. Now, sculptors often use lasers and computers in their work.
- To make a sculpture from metal, the sculptor makes a mold and pours melted metal into the mold. This method is called casting.
- Sculpture parts may also be welded, glued, or otherwise attached to one other to complete a sculpture.
- Ice sculptures are popular decorations at weddings and other special events.

Bookmark # 42-4

MISCELLANEOUS ARTS
Ballet

- A ballet is a play in which music, dance, and mime tell the story. Some of the best-known ballets are *Giselle, The Nutcracker, The Sleeping Beauty,* and *Swan Lake.*
- A composer writes the music for a ballet, and the choreographer develops the movements for the ballet dancers using five basic positions.

Bookmark # 42-5

MISCELLANEOUS ARTS
Elements of a Play

- A comedy is a humorous play that has a happy ending.
- A tragedy is a play that has a sad ending.
- An act is a primary division of a play.
- A scene is a division of an act.
- A setting is the location in which the story takes place.
- A cast of characters is the people involved in the story. A role is a character an actor plays.
- Dialogue is the words the characters say.
- Stage directions give hints for actors and set designers to make the story more believable.

Bookmark # 42-6

MISCELLANEOUS ARTS
Pantomime

- A genuine pantomime is a play based on a fairy tale, not the silent performance of a mime actor. True pantomimes are most often performed near Christmas.
- The main character in a pantomime is usually a young woman, often played by a man dressed in women's clothes to be funny. The "bad guy" in a pantomime is always very evil.
- A pantomime can also be a form of entertainment in which the actors tell the story without words and often without props. The actors use only gestures and expressions.

Bookmark # 42-7

MISCELLANEOUS ARTS
Puppets and Marionettes

- The earliest marionettes were called shadow puppets. The puppets were cut in silhouette form out of stiff paper or cardboard. Later, the marionettes were carved from wood or made of baked clay.
- Hand puppets were created to allow more complicated movements that less skilled people could make.
- Punch and Judy are puppets that became famous in the late 1600s. A Jack-in-the-box toy was once known as a "Punch-in-the-box. The phrase "pleased as Punch" also refers to the puppet.

Bookmark # 42-8

MISCELLANEOUS ARTS
Statues

- Leonardo da Vinci started working on a statue of Francesco Sforza. The invasion of French soldiers prevented him from completing the work. The soldiers used the statue for archery practice and destroyed it. No known statue by da Vinci is known to exist.
- Michelangelo once walked through a courtyard of a cathedral in Florence, Italy. He saw a huge block of marble that no one else wanted. Michelangelo took the marble and spent 17 months completing his statue *David*. He finished the statue on January 25, 1504.

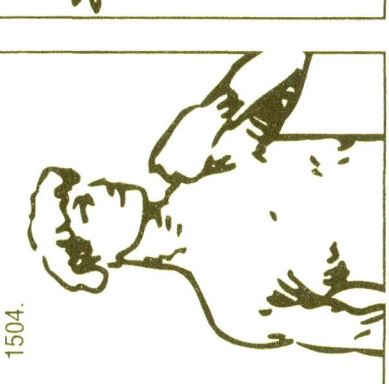

MUSIC
General Music

- The song most frequently sung in the world is "Happy Birthday to You," written by Patty and Mildred Hill in 1893.
- More Americans play the piano than any other musical instrument.
- MTV (Music Television), launched in 1981, was the first TV station to feature only video music.

MUSIC
Music Influenced by African Americans

- Motown—catchy tunes often featuring African-American musicians; originated in Detroit; popular in the 1960s
- rap—features a drum machine, scratching a needle of a record player across a record, and rhythmic talking; popular in the 1980s
- reggae—features a pulsating beat and often a political or religious message in the words; originated on the island of Jamaica and made popular by the late Bob Marley
- spirituals—songs with a religious theme originally sung by slaves

MUSIC
Classical Music

- Chamber music is written to be played or sung by a small group.
- A symphony is written to be performed by an orchestra.
- An opera is a play in which the words are sung to music.
- Bach paid for his education by singing in a choir.
- Beethoven played piano in public at age 8 and published compositions at age 10.
- Chopin first played a concerto in public at age 9.
- Mozart composed minuets at age 3.
- Schubert was seriously composing by the age of 11.

MUSIC
Vivaldi's Four Seasons

Antonio Vivaldi was a priest in Italy in the early 1700s, but asthma left him unable to say Mass. He became a music director of an orphanage for girls. He composed a piece of music for violin and orchestra to celebrate spring, summer, autumn, and winter. He appropriately titled it *Four Seasons*. Each season in the composition has three movements.

SECTION X: ARTS AND ENTERTAINMENT | 129

MUSIC
Folk Music

- traditional folk—music passed down for generations; often many versions of the same song are known
- blues—based on African-American music; often has a "life is hard" message
- country and western—usually has heavy use of stringed instruments; sometimes teasingly referred to as "drinking and cheating" music
- gospel—has a religious theme and features elements of blues, jazz, and spirituals
- shanties or sea shanties—popular among sailors

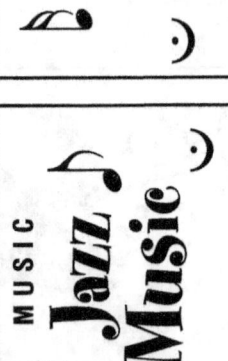

Bookmark # 43-5

MUSIC
Jazz Music

- Jazz music began in the southern United States. The music of former slaves first became popular in the late 1800s. The early jazz music incorporated the rhythms and beats of African music.
- A jazz band usually has between 4 and 10 musicians. Primary instruments of jazz are trumpet, trombone, clarinet, saxophone, drums, piano, and tuba. Other instruments include bass guitar, violin, and flute.
- Jazz music is often upbeat and includes improvising (making up music on the spot).

Bookmark # 43-6

MUSIC
Rock Music

- disco—dance music with a heavy beat; popular in the mid- to late-1970s
- folk rock—combines rock music and folk music; words often have a political message; popular in the early 1960s
- glam rock—features fabulous costumes and elaborate staging of concerts; popular in the early 1970s
- heavy metal—very loud music, often using feedback; dates from the late 1960s
- punk rock—music meant to be shocking; popular in the 1970s

Bookmark # 43-7

MUSIC
Keyboard Instruments

- Keyboard instruments have keys that produce sound when struck. Some types of keyboard instruments include piano, organ, accordion, carillon, and celesta.
- The first pipe organ was made in Greece in 250 B.C. The organ, with its small row of 20 pipes, worked by water pressure.
- An organ in England 1,000 years ago had 400 pipes and needed 70 men to pump its 26 bellows. One listener described the sound it made as "unbearable."

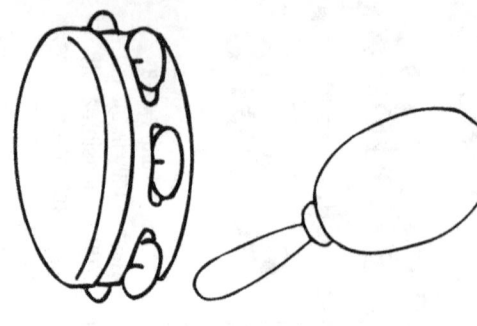

Bookmark # 43-8

MUSIC
Percussion Instruments

- The word *percussion* literally means "hitting." Players strike a percussion instrument with their hands or something else to make sounds. Some percussion instruments are shaken to make sounds.
- Some examples of percussion instruments include castanets, chimes, cymbals, drums, glockenspiel, gong, tambourine, triangle, and xylophone.

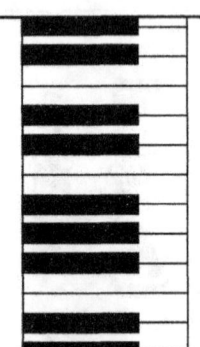

Bookmark # 43-9

MUSIC
Drums

- A bass drum emits a deep low sound when hit with a mallet.
- Bongo drums are played by striking them with the palms of the hands.
- A snare drum, also known as a side drum, is played with sticks.
- A timpani, also known as a kettledrum, is struck with a hard or a soft mallet to produce different sounds. A timpani is the only drum that can play actual notes.

Bookmark # 43-10

MUSIC
Stringed Instruments

- About two-thirds of the instruments in an orchestra are stringed instruments.
- Music is usually created on a stringed instrument by drawing the fingers or a bow across the strings, or plucking the strings with the fingers.
- Examples of stringed instruments include banjo, cello, double bass, guitar, harp, viola, and violin.
- The banjo is the only true musical instrument that began in the United States.
- Antonio Stradivarius made violins in the late 1600s and early 1700s. Some of those violins are still being played today.

Bookmark # 43-11

MUSIC
Wind Instruments

- Wind instruments produce sound by the forced vibration from air (usually breath) in a pipe or tube.
- The first wind instrument was likely a flute made from bamboo or other hollow wood or even hollow bones. Primitive cave dwellers were known to have made flutes.
- Some examples of woodwind instruments include the bassoon, clarinet, flute, and oboe.
- Some examples of brass wind instruments include the horn, trombone, trumpet, and tuba.

Bookmark # 43-12

HOBBIES AND FUN
Amusement Parks

- The first Ferris wheel had 36 cars that each held 60 passengers. Up to 2,160 people could ride at the same time.
- Nagashima Spaland in Japan has a 300-foot tall roller coaster. The coaster is more than 8,000 feet long (about a mile and a half) and goes more than 90 miles per hour.

Bookmark # 44-1

HOBBIES AND FUN
Autograph Album

Popular autograph album entries:

Don't kiss by the garden gate
'Cuz love is blind
But the neighbors ain't

....

Remember the North
Remember the South
Remember me
And my big mouth

....

Roses are red
Violets are blue
Give me some money
And I'll love you

....

2 good
2 be
4 gotten

....

See you in the comics

....

Yours 'til the butter flies

Bookmark # 44-2

SECTION X: ARTS AND ENTERTAINMENT | 131

HOBBIES AND FUN
Boy and Girl Scouts of America

- Sir Robert S. S. Baden-Powell wrote a book called *Aids to Scouting*. A boy he taught to be a scout helped William D. Boyce while he was visiting England. Boyce returned to the United States and started the Boy Scouts of America on February 8, 1910.
- In 1909, Sir Robert Baden-Powell's sister founded the Girl Guides in England. On March 12, 1912, Mrs. Juliett Low of Savannah, Georgia, invited 11 girls to a meeting in her unused stable. That was the first meeting of the Girl Guides (later called Girl Scouts) in America.

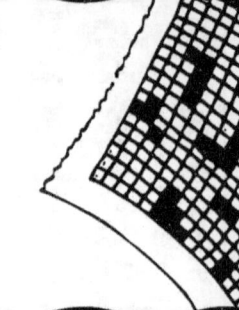

Bookmark # 44-3

HOBBIES AND FUN
Celebrity Autographs

- People will pay large amounts of money for autographs, no matter what's been signed—even canceled checks.
- Elvis Presley's autograph has sold for more than $100.
- A letter written by Button Gwinnet, one of the men who signed the Declaration of Independence, brought over $50,000 at an auction.

Bookmark # 44-4

HOBBIES AND FUN
Chess

- The original form of chess was invented in India about 1,300 years ago. The names of the pieces and how they move changed from time to time and from country to country.
- The number of possible first moves on each side is 318,979,564,000 ways. The 10 opening moves include 170 septillion (170 followed by 8 sets of "000") possible ways.
- Chess sets have been made from all kinds of materials, in a wide variety of sizes, and with many types of playing pieces, including book and movie characters.

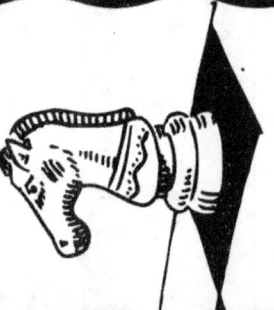

Bookmark # 44-5

HOBBIES AND FUN
Circuses

- Bill Ricketts gave the first circus performance in Philadelphia on April 3, 1793.
- Early circus acts included unusual animals, athletic competitions, and races. Many people found watching the circus come to town and set up as interesting as seeing the performance.
- Barnum and Bailey's circus needed more than 50 railroad cars to move it from town to town.
- Circus performances used to be held in tents owned by the traveling circuses. Now, most circuses are held in auditoriums.

Bookmark # 44-6

HOBBIES AND FUN
Crossword Puzzles

- The first crossword puzzle appeared in England in the 19th century.
- More than 40,000 copies of the first crossword puzzle book, published in the 1920s, sold within three months. The book of 50 puzzles sold for $1.35.
- An average *Times* crossword puzzle contains 120 white squares. The number of possible solutions using any of the 26 letters in any square is about 24,873 followed by 74 sets of "000."
- Someone who makes up crossword puzzles is called a cruciverbalist.

Bookmark # 44-7

HOBBIES AND FUN

Dice

- The word *dice* comes from the Latin word *dare*, meaning "to give."
- The two numbers on opposite sides of a die add up to seven.
- Dice may be square because Earth was once thought to be square.
- The six sides of dice represent the six realms of the universe: animal, plant, mineral, human, psychic, and divine (God).

Bookmark # 44-8

HOBBIES AND FUN

Greeting Cards

- The first greeting cards are thought to have been valentines from the Middle Ages.
- Louis Prang started printing Christmas cards in 1875. The cost of $1 to $5 each was very expensive at the time.
- Greeting cards can reflect society at the time they're printed. Cards that feature various TV, comic strip, or historical events show the popular culture at the time.

Bookmark # 44-9

HOBBIES AND FUN

Jokes

Q. What's gray on the inside and clear on the outside?
A. An elephant in a plastic bag.

·······

Q. What's worse than a centipede with a sprained ankle?
A. A giraffe with a sore throat.

·······

Q. Why did the fool take a ruler to bed?
A. He wanted to see how long he slept.

·······

Knock, knock.
Who's there?
Harry.
Harry who?
Harry up and open the door; it's cold out here!

Bookmark # 44-10

HOBBIES AND FUN

Jump Ropes

- Jump ropes originated thousands of years ago. Someone may have realized that jumping over a vine was fun.
- Jump ropes were once used in planting or harvesting seasons. One belief was that the crops would grow only as high as the planter could jump after he planted the fields.
- One jump rope rhyme:
  Cinderella
  Dressed in yellow
  Went downtown
  To kiss a fellow
  It was foggy
  She kissed a doggy
  How many kisses 'til she got soggy?
  1, 2, 3, 4, 5, ...

178, 179, 180,

Bookmark # 44-11

HOBBIES AND FUN

Playing Cards

- The first known playing cards appeared about 1,300 years ago. Playing cards similar to the cards today first appeared about 900 years ago in China.
- Benjamin Franklin was one of the first to manufacture playing cards in America.
- The design on Bicycle playing cards changes as the style of bicycles changes.
- The number of different ways a pack of 52 cards can lay in a stack totals 80,660 followed by 21 sets of "000."

Bookmark # 44-12

SECTION X: ARTS AND ENTERTAINMENT | 133

HOBBIES AND FUN
Postcards

- Postcards were popular between 1900-1914, before telephones were in use and mail was inexpensive. In 1904, about 2,000,000 postcards were mailed each day. Many people collected postcards and sent postcards with messages such as "Here's another card for your collection."
- More than 8,000 different postcards are related to Abraham Lincoln in some way.

Bookmark # 44-13

HOBBIES AND FUN
Riddles

Riddles are brain teasers that are sometimes funny and sometimes a test of wits. Some examples are

Q. What's black and white and red all over?

A. An embarrassed zebra.

Q. What goes up to the house, but never goes in?

A. A sidewalk.

Bookmark # 44-14

HOBBIES AND FUN
Stamps

- Great Britain issued the first stamp in 1840. The use of stamps allowed the sender to pay for delivery in advance. Before then, the person who received the letter had to pay for the letter—at a cost more than that to buy a restaurant meal.
- The first "lick-and-stick" postage stamps in the United States were made in 1842. They were called "famous Penny Blacks." Now, most stamps are self-stick; they no longer need to be licked.
- No living person is allowed to be depicted on a U.S. postage stamp.

Bookmark # 44-15

TOYS
Balls

- The first "balls" may have been the heads of enemies.
- Stone balls date back to 3000-2000 B.C. Balls made of wood, cork, animal skin stuffed with grass, or other materials have also been around for thousands of years.
- Most balls have been made of rubber or other human-made materials since 1839, when rubber was invented.
- Balls have been a part of combat, rain dance rituals, church ceremonies, romance customs, and fortune telling, among other uses.

Bookmark # 45-1

TOYS
Frisbee

- The beginning of flying disks can be traced back to Ancient Greece. Items such as saw blades, pie plates, and film reel canister lids have been used as flying disks.
- Wham-O released the "Pluto Platter" in 1957. The toy was named for the planet because the world was in the middle of a UFO craze and the toy looked like a flying saucer. The name of the toy was later changed to Frisbee.
- In 1968, the U.S. Navy spent nearly $400,000 to test Frisbees to use for keeping flares in the air longer.

Bookmark # 45-2

134 | BOOKMARKS ACROSS THE CURRICULUM

TOYS

Raggedy Ann

- Johnny Gruelle wrote the famous "Raggedy Ann" stories beginning in 1918. The doll was manufactured to promote the stories.
- A genuine Raggedy Ann doll has a heart inscribed with the words "I Love You." The original hearts were made of candy, but are now made of plastic or wood.

Bookmark # 45-7

TOYS

Marbles

- Marbles come in many different sizes and materials, such as alabaster, clay, glass, metals, and bone.
- Roman emperor Augustus Caesar stopped to play marbles with any boys he saw playing with them.
- George Washington, John Adams, Thomas Jefferson, and Abraham Lincoln were all avid marble players and collectors.

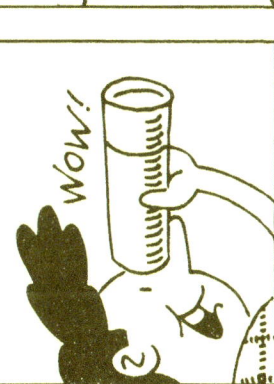

Bookmark # 45-6

TOYS

Kites

- Kites have been used as weapons and to study the weather. Kites were once thought to be able to drive away spirits.
- In 200 B.C., a Chinese general used a kite to measure the distance between his army and the city he wanted to conquer.
- In 1752, Benjamin Franklin used a kite to prove that the electricity is the same in lightning and on the ground.
- In 1853, Sir George Caley constructed a double kite to ride. He was too afraid to fly it himself and made his coachman be the pilot.

Bookmark # 45-5

TOYS

Kaleidoscope

- A kaleidoscope is a tube made with mirrors and fragments of colored glass or other materials to make symmetrical patterns. The movement of the kaleidoscope will change the patterns.
- Kaleidoscopes are named for a Greek word meaning "an instrument with which we can see things of beautiful form."
- A Scottish scientist named Sir David Brewster rediscovered the fun and fascination of a kaleidoscope. He patented the object in 1817. Kaleidoscopes didn't become popular until he published a book about them two years later.

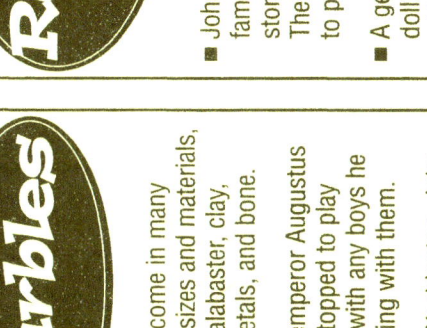

Bookmark # 45-4

TOYS

Hula Hoop

- The Hula Hoop is named for hula dancers. Other names manufacturers considered for the toy included "Twirl-A-Hoop" and "Swing-A-Hoop."
- Within four months from the time Hula Hoops appeared on the *Dinah Shore Show* on TV, 25 million hoops were sold.

Bookmark # 45-3

SECTION X: ARTS AND ENTERTAINMENT | 135

TOYS
Savings and "Piggy" Banks

- Simple forms of savings banks called "money boxes" were found in ancient graves in England. Slots in the boxes allowed coins to be slipped inside easily.
- Originally, piggy banks weren't intended to be in the shape of pigs. Customers would ask for a "pig bank," meaning a bank made out of pig clay. They'd get a bank in the shape of a pig.

Bookmark # 45-8

TOYS
Silly Putty

- No Silly Putty could be manufactured during the Korean War because the government banned synthetic rubber for anything but defense uses.
- A woman gave the Apollo 8 astronauts a lot of Silly Putty. She thought they could use the toy for entertainment and to stick tools in place during weightlessness.

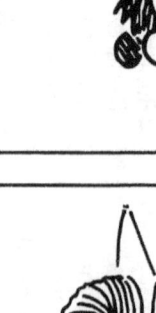

Bookmark # 45-9

TOYS
Slinky

- Vietnam communication soldiers tossed Slinkys over high tree branches to use as makeshift radio antennas.
- Astronauts on a space shuttle voyage discovered that zero gravity makes a Slinky become a continuously moving wave.

Bookmark # 45-10

TOYS
Teddy Bear

During a hunting trip in 1902, Theodore Roosevelt refused to kill a bear cub and took it home with him instead. Clifford Berryman drew a cartoon about the event. Toy maker Morris Michtom saw the cartoon and was inspired to make toy bears. Michtom got permission from Roosevelt to name his toys "Teddy's Bears."

Bookmark # 45-11

TOYS
Yo-Yo

- Yo-yos originated in China about 3,000 years ago. At that time, yo-yos were made with two disks of ivory with silk cord wound around a connecting peg.
- Hunters in the Philippines in the 16th century used large yo-yos as weapons. The yo-yos could be thrown or the string could be used to trip someone.
- "Yo-yo" means "come-come" in the Filipino language.
- For several weeks in 1932, about 35,000 yo-yos a day were being sold in Britain.

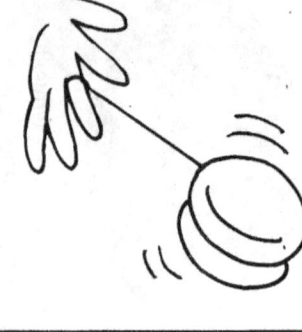

Bookmark # 45-12

SPORTS
BASEBALL

- Before 1845, bases were made of posts or stakes arranged in a *U* shape.
- Home plate has five sides instead of four like the other bases to help umpires spot the location of the ball as it passes over the plate.
- The pitcher's mound was likely supposed to be only 60 feet from home plate instead of the 60_ feet that it is. Sloppy handwriting is blamed for the error.

Bookmark # 46-1

SPORTS
BASEBALL GAMES

- Egyptians held batting contests as early as 5000 B.C. They even had fielders to catch fly balls.
- The first official baseball game took place in Hoboken, New Jersey, on June 19, 1846. The New York Club beat the Knickerbockers by a score of 23-1. One of the Knickerbockers players was fined 6 cents for swearing.
- The Cincinnati Red Stockings became the first professional baseball team. They won their first 92 games.
- During the 1886 World Series, players committed 63 errors.

Bookmark # 46-2

SPORTS
BASKETBALL

- About 3,000 years ago, the Olmec tribe of Mexico played a game in which players threw a round object through a ring.
- The first set of basketball regulations appeared in January 1892, the year after Dr. James Naismith invented the modern version of the game. He attached peach baskets to the railing of a gym balcony. Whenever someone got a ball in the basket, play had to be stopped while someone retrieved the ball.
- The first basketball teams had nine players.

Bookmark # 46-3

SPORTS
FOOTBALL

- Before helmets, players let their hair grow long to absorb shocks.
- During 1905, 18 players were killed and 159 permanently injured in college football games. President Theodore Roosevelt created the National Collegiate Athletic Association to develop regulations to make the sport safer.
- John Heisman, for whom the trophy is named, is credited with introducing the terms "hep" and "hike" to football in 1898.

Bookmark # 46-4

SPORTS
GOLF

- The game of golf similar to the game today is said to have started in Scotland when a shepherd used a crook to knock pebbles through the air. When one fell into a rabbit hole, a friend challenged him to do it again.
- Before 1850, golf balls were made of "as many feathers as would fill the brim of a top hat" and covered in leather.
- A golf ball has 336 dimples.
- Immediately after being struck off the tee, a golf ball moves about 150 miles per hour.

Bookmark # 46-5

SECTION X: ARTS AND ENTERTAINMENT | 137

SPORTS
GYMNASTICS

- Gymnastics originated in Ancient Greece, where exercise was a major part of life.
- The word *gymnastics* is derived from a Greek word meaning "to exercise naked."
- Ancient Romans made gymnastics a part of their military training.
- A gymnast requires a great amount of strength, flexibility, and agility.
- Gymnastics competitions include floor exercises, parallel bars, uneven parallel bars, horizontal bar, side horse, long horse, and rings.
- A floor exercise routine performed to music takes place in an area about 41 square feet.

Bookmark # 46-6

SPORTS
HOCKEY

- Hockey's name comes from the Old French word *hoquet*, which means "hooked stick." The modern French word *hoquet* means "hiccups."
- The modern game of hockey started out as a field game in England about 1850. The game was first played on the ice in the 1860s.
- The first organized hockey game in the United States took place on October 28, 1928, at the Germantown Cricket Club in Philadelphia, Pennsylvania.
- Some hockey players tap the goalie on the shinguards before a game for luck.

Bookmark # 46-7

SPORTS
ICE SKATING

- Ice skating may have been invented when someone slipped on a piece of bone on the ice the way someone would slip on a banana peel. The person realized traveling across the ice on a piece of bone could be faster, easier, and more fun than walking.
- In 1396, a Dutch girl named Siedwi became disabled after a bad fall while wearing ice skates. She then devoted herself to others and became the patron saint of ice skaters.
- A dancer named Jackson Haines developed figure skating. He is known as the father of modern figure skating.

Bookmark # 46-8

SPORTS
ROLLER SKATES

- In 1760, Joseph Merlin of Belgium built and demonstrated "a pair of skates." He played a violin while he skated, but lost control of his movements and crashed into a mirror.
- In the 1880s, roller skating on Sundays became so popular that people stopped going to church. Sermons at the time often included the message that skating was "evil."

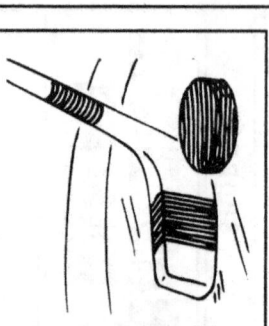

Bookmark # 46-9

SPORTS
SCUBA DIVING

- The term scuba stands for "**S**elf-**C**ontained **U**nderwater **B**reathing **A**pparatus."
- During traditional scuba diving, divers breathe air from a tank. When the diver exhales, the air is released into the water.
- A new type of scuba equipment recycles exhaled air back into oxygen to enable divers to stay under water longer even though they carry a smaller amount of oxygen.

Bookmark # 46-10

138 | BOOKMARKS ACROSS THE CURRICULUM

SPORTS
SNOW SKIING

- A ski at least 4,000 years old was found in Sweden.
- The first skiing competitions were tests of speed, but tests of endurance were quickly added.
- The first known cross-country ski race took place in Norway in 1843.
- Downhill skiing for speed is considered the fastest sport without animal assistance or a motor.
- Skiing didn't become popular in the United States until after the 1932 Winter Olympics held at New York's Lake Placid.

Bookmark # 46-11

SPORTS
SOCCER

- In most parts of the world, soccer is known as "football."
- An early form of soccer may have been played in Rome and Greece about 1,750 years ago.
- During the 14th century, King Edward III wanted to ban the game of soccer because players spent too much time on soccer and not enough time on archery. That didn't stop people from playing soccer.
- Hundreds of people who have attended soccer games have been killed when fans have gotten too upset about the officials' calls or losing a game.

Bookmark # 46-12

SPORTS
SURFING

- A ceramic figurine dating back thousands of years ago shows a surfer on a short board.
- Captain James Cook saw Polynesians surfing in canoes in 1777.
- Before entering the water, surfers used to sing hymns or chant as a way of asking the gods for good waves.
- Calvinist missionaries from Boston who visited Hawaii in 1821 declared surfing sinful because surfers wore few clothes. People started using their surfboards as benches and tables. Surfing became popular again in the early 1900s.

Bookmark # 46-13

SPORTS
TENNIS

- The first games of tennis may have been played in monasteries.
- The game of tennis may have been named for the French word *tenez*, which means "play."
- Tennis players once asked their servants to hit the first ball in a game. The term "service" may have started from that practice.
- The term "love" may be from the French word *l'oeuf*, which means "egg"—shaped like a goose egg or a zero (0).
- The tennis term "deuce" may be from *a deux*, meaning two consecutive points needed to win.

Bookmark # 46-14

SECTION X: ARTS AND ENTERTAINMENT | 139

Students or educators may use the following blank bookmarks to create bookmarks for supplementary material not covered in this book, to reinforce particular material a student finds difficult, or simply for fun. The blank bookmarks may also be given to students to design their own bookmarks.

Bookmarks Across the Curriculum

References

Ardley, Bridget and Neil Ardley, *The Random House Book of 1001 Questions and Answers*. Random House, 1989.

Ashabranner, Brent, *Always to Remember: The Story of the Vietnam Veterans Memorial*. Dodd, Mead, 1988.

Asimov, Isaac, *Unidentified Flying Objects*. Dell Yearling, 1989.

Ayer, Eleanor, *Our Flag*. The Millbrook Press, 1992.

Bett, Henry, *The Games of Children: Their Origin and History*. Detroit: Singing Tree Press, 1968.

Blacknall, Carolyn, *Sally Ride: America's First Woman in Space*. Minneapolis, MN: Dillon Press, 1984.

Botermans, Jack, Tony Burrett, Pietervan Delft, and Carla van Splunteren, *The World of Games*. Facts on File, 1987.

Brent, Isabelle, *An Alphabet of Animals*. Little Brown, 1993.

Brookfield, Karen, *Eyewitness Series: Book*. Alfred A. Knopf, 1993.

Brown, Marion Marsh, *Sacajawea: Indian Interpreter to Lewis and Clark*. Children's Press, 1988.

Burnie, David, *Eyewitness Series: Plant*. Alfred A. Knopf, 1989.

Cranfield, Ingrid, *Animal World*. New York: Dorset Press, 1991.

Curtis, Neil and Michael Allaby, *Visual Factfinder: Planet Earth*. New York: Kingfisher Books, 1993.

Daniels, Roger, *The Decision to Relocate the Japanese Americans*. Malabar, FL: Robert E. Krieger Publishing Company, 1975.

Douglas, George William, *The American Book of Days*. H. W. Wilson, 1948.

Eastman, Charles A., *Indian Heroes and Great Chieftans*. University of Nebraska Press, 1991.

Elliott, Lawrence, *George Washington Carver: The Man Who Overcame*. Prentice-Hall, 1966.

Farndon, John, *Eyewitness Question and Answer Book*. Dorling Kindersley, 1993.

Ferris, Jeri, *Walking the Road to Freedom: A Story About Sojourner Truth*. Carolrhoda, 1988.

Fisher, Leonard Everett, *The Alamo*. Holiday House, 1987.

—————, *Ellis Island: Gateway to the New World*. Holiday House, 1986.

Fletcher, Christine, *100 Keys: Names Across the Land*. Abingdon, 1973.

Fritz, Jean, *Make Way for Sam Houston*. Putnam, 1986.

—————, *Who's That Stepping on Plymouth Rock?* Coward, McCann 1975.

Gallagher, Rachel, *Games in the Street*. Four Winds, 1976.

Goldwyn, Martin M., *How a Fly Walks Upside Down . . . and Other Curious Facts*. Secaucus, NJ: Citadel Press, 1979.

Goodenough, Simon, Tim Dowley, Michael March, Janet Sachs, and Suzie Siddons, *1500 Fascinating Facts*. London: Octopus Books, 1983.

Graham, Ian, *Motorcycles: Built for Speed*. Steck-Vaughn, 1999.

Grant, Reg, series editor, *Unsolved Mysteries of the Past*. Reader's Digest Association, 1991.

Handlin, Oscar, *Statue of Liberty*. Newsweek, 1971.

Hargrove, Jim, *The Story of Watergate*. Children's Press, 1988.
Harvey, Edmund H. Jr., editor, *Reader's Digest Book of Facts*. Reader's Digest, 1987.
Hook, Sue and Angela Royston, *A First Atlas*. Scholastic, 1995.
Hulme, Joy N. and Donna W. Guthrie, *How to Write, Recite, and Delight in All Kinds of Poetry*. The Millbrook Press, 1996.
January, Brendan, *The New York Public Library Amazing Explorers: A Book of Answers for Kids*. John Wiley, 2001.
Johnson, Linda Carlson, *Our National Symbols*. The Millbrook Press, 1992.
Katz, William Loren, *An Album of the Great Depression*. Franklin Watts, 1978.
Kaye, Marvin, *A Toy Is Born*. New York: Stein and Day, 1973.
Kent, Zachary, *The Story of John Brown's Raid on Harpers Ferry*. Children's Press, 1988.
—————, *The Story of the Surrender at Appomattox Court House*. Children's Press, 1987.
Ketchum, William C. Jr., *Toys and Games*. New York: Cooper-Hewitt Museum: The Smithsonian Institution's National Museum of Design, 1981.
Kettelkamp, Larry, *Dreams*. William Morrow, 1968.
Lee, Martin, *Paul Revere*. Franklin Watts, 1987.
Levey, Judith S., editor, *The World Almanac for Kids 1996*. Funk & Wagnalls, 1995.
Lindsay, Rae, *The Left-Handed Book*. Franklin Watts, 1980.
Lomask, Milton, *Great Lives: Invention and Technology*. Scribner, 1991.
Louis, David, *2201 Fascinating Facts*. Greenwich House/Crown, 1983.
Lyttle, Richard B., *The Games They Played: Sports in History*. Atheneum, 1982.
Marron, Carol, *Yellowstone*. New York: Crestwood House, 1988.
Maynard, Christopher, *Amazing Animal Facts*. Knopf, 1993.
McLoone-Basta, Margo and Alice Siegel, *The Kids' World Almanac of Records and Facts*. World Almanac Publications, 1985.
Meyers, James, *Jumbo Amazing Question and Answer Book*. New York: Playmore, Inc., 1990.
Miers, Earl Schenck, *Our Fifty States*. Grosset and Dunlap, 1961.
Millington, Roger, *Crossword Puzzles: Their History and Their Cult*. Thomas Nelson, 1974.
Milner, Dr. Angela, consulting editor, *Discoveries Library: Dinosaurs*. Time-Life Books, 1995.
O'Neill, Richard and Antonia D. Bryan, *Facts America: Presidents of the United States*. New York: Smithmark Publishers, 1992.
Parsons, Alexandra, *Amazing Birds*. Knopf, 1990.
Pasachoff, Jay M., *Peterson First Guide to Astronomy*. Houghton Mifflin, 1988.
Peterson, Helen Stone, *Susan B. Anthony: Pioneer in Woman's Rights*. Champaign, IL: Garrard Publishing Company, 1971.
Pierce, Edith Gray, *Horace Mann: Our Nation's First Educator*. Lerner, 1972.
Pyke, Dr. Magnus, *Weird and Wonderful Science Facts*. New York: Sterling Publishing, 1984.
Retan, Walter, *101 Wacky Facts About Snakes and Reptiles*. Scholastic, 1991.
Robinson, Nancy, *Buffalo Bill*. Franklin Watts, 1991.
Rose, Dr. Marie, *Discoveries Library: The Human Body*. Time Life Books, 1997.

Rothaus, James R., *Crazy Horse: War Chief of the Oglala 1841-1887*. Creative Education, 1987.

Scheffel, Richard L., editor, *ABC's of Nature*. Reader's Digest, 1984.

Settel, Joanne and Nancy Baggett, *Why Do Cats' Eyes Glow in the Dark?* Atheneum, 1988.

Seuling, Barbara, *Elephants Can't Jump and Other Freaky Facts About Animals*. Lodestar/Dutton, 1985.

St. George, Judith, *The Mount Rushmore Story*. Putnam, 1985.

St. Pierre, Stephanie, *Our National Anthem*. The Millbrook Press, 1992.

Staple, Michelle and Linda Gamlin, *The Random House Book of 1001 Questions and Answers About Animals*. Random House, 1990.

Steele, Anne, *Egyptian Pyramids*. New York: The Bookwright Press, 1990.

Stein, R. Conrad, *The Story of Little Bighorn*. Children's Press, 1983.

—————, *The Story of the Great Depression*. Children's Press, 1985.

—————, *The Story of Valley Forge*. Children's Press, 1985.

Stewart, Jeffrey C., *1001 Things Everyone Should Know About African American History*. Doubleday, 1996.

Sublette, Guen, *The Book of Days*. New York: Perigee/Berkley Publishing Group, 1996.

Sutton, Richard, *Eyewitness Series: Car*. Knopf, 1990.

Trefil, James, *Sharks Have No Bones*. Fireside/Simon & Schuster, 1992.

Tulin, Melissa S., *Aardvarks to Zebras*. New York: MJF Books, 1995.

Waricha, Jean, *101 Wacky Facts About Bugs and Spiders*. Scholastic, 1991.

Waters, Kate, *The Story of the White House*. Scholastic, 1971.

Wingate, Philippa, *The Internet for Beginners*. London: Usborne Publishing, 1997.

Zadra, Dan, *Daniel Boone: In the Wilderness 1734-1820*. Creative Education, 1988.

—————, *Robert E. Lee: The South's Great General 1807-1870*. Creative Education, 1988.

Zauner, Phyllis and Lou Zauner, *California Gold: Story of the Rush to Riches*. Sonoma, CA: Zanel Publications, 1980.

Zim, Herbert S. and Robert H. Baker, revised and updated by Mark R. Chartrand, Golden Guide *Stars*. Golden Press, 1985.

Internet Resources:

"The Bill of Rights." <http://www.politicalgifts.com/politicalgifts/billofrights.html>.

"The First Ladies of the United States of America." <http://www.whitehouse.gov/history/firstladies/>.

"Four Major Classification Schemes," from *International Encyclopedia of Information and Library Science*. John Feather and Paul Sturges, editors, 1997. <http://alexia.lis.uiuc.edu/course/fall 1998/lis380/week07/cls_scheme.html>.

"Greek and Roman Mythological Gods." <http://www.geocities.com/Athens/Troy/2774/mythgods.html>.

"Police Canine Training Standard." New York State Division of Criminal Justice Services Bureau of Municipal Police. <http://www.policek9.com/Standards/nystand/nystand.html>.

"The Presidents of the United States." <http://www.whitehouse.gov/history/presidents/index.html>. (This address leads the searcher to each president.)

"State Capitals and Other Facts." <http://www.mount-merici.pvt.k12.me.us/merillca.htm>.
"Vice Presidents of the United States." Information provided by Grolier from "The American Presidents." Grolier, 1995.
<http://www.usahistory.com/presidents/vicepres.htm>.
"Visible Light Waves." <http://imagers.gsfc.nasa.gov/ems/visible.html>.
"What Are Holograms Used For?" Frank DeFreitas.
<http://www.holoworld.com/holo/quest6.html>.
"What Is an Invertebrate?" <http://www.geology.wisc.edu/~museum/invertinfo.html>.
"What Is Lightning?" Lightning Information Center at the National Weather Service of Melbourne, Florida. <http://www.srh.noaa.gov/mlb/ltgcenter/whatis.html>.
"When Is ASL ASL?" Roger Carver, M.Ed.
<http://www.deafworldweb.org/pub/a/whenasl.html>.

The following Web sites were used to verify a variety of information from other sources:
<http://encarta.msn.com >
<http://howstuffworks.lycos.com>

Index

Index references are to bookmark numbers.
Entries in **bold** type are the main subjects of the bookmarks.

A

Abraham 35-6
Adams, Abigail 16-18, 31-2
Adams, John 9-16, 14-33, 16-18, 31-1, **31-2**, 31-6, 45-6
Adams, John Quincy 31-6
Adams, Louisa 31-6
adding 7-5
adjectives 3-2
Administration of Justice Act 10-4
adverbs 3-4
Africa 12-1, **12-2**
Agnew, Spiro T. 31-36
airplanes 40-1
Alabama 14-2
Alamo 16-3
Alaska 10-18, 14-1, **14-3**
albatross 26-5
Alcatraz 16-4
Alexander the Great 37-1
alligator 27-3
alliteration 4-4
alphabet 1-1
American Library Association 1-8
American Sign Language 34-1
amphibians 27-1
amusement parks 44-1
Andersen, Hans Christian 36-2
ant 29-2
Antarctica 12-1, **12-3**
Anthony, Susan B. 33-1
antonyms 4-1
Apollo Project 40-7
apostrophe 2-3
Appomattox, Virgina 10-17
April 9-5
April Fool's Day 9-22
arachnids 30-1
Arizona 14-4
Arjun, Guru 35-8
Arkansas 14-5
armadillo 25-1
Armistice Day 9-36
Armstrong, Neil 9-8
Arnold, Benedict 33-2
Arthur, Chester Alan 31-20, **31-21**
Arthur, Ellen 31-21

articles (figure of speech) 3-3
artificial limbs 23-1
Asia 12-1, **12-4**
assonance 4-5
Atahualpa 32-8
Atlanta, Georgia 10-16
Atlantis 36-7
atmosphere 18-2
August 9-9
auroras (northern lights) 19-8
Australia (continent) 12-1, **12-5**
Australia (country) 13-2
autograph albums 44-2
autographs, celebrity 44-4
automobiles, early 40-2
automobile's working parts 40-3
avalanches 19-1
averages 7-15

B

Bach, Johann 43-3
Baden-Powell, Robert S. 44-3
Balboa, Vasco de 32-1, 32-8
bald eagle 26-6
ballet 42-5
balls 45-1
bananas 21-4
Barkley, Alben W. 31-32
barnacle 28-3
Barnum and Bailey's circus 44-6
Bartholdi, Frederic Auguste 16-14
baseball 46-1
baseball games 46-2
basketball 46-3
bat 25-2
bathtubs 41-1
batteries 41-2
Battle of Brandywine 9-28
beards 37-1
bee 29-3
Beethoven, Ludwig von 43-3
beetle 29-4
Bermuda Triangle 36-8
Berner, E. C. 38-2
Berryman, Clifford 45-11
Bible 1-3, 19-10, 35-2
bibliography 1-4

bicycles 40-4
Bigfoot 36-9
Bill of Rights 11-3
Bingham Library for Youth 1-9
bird nests 26-2
birds 26-1
Blanchard, Jean Pierre 40-5
Blarney Stone 16-5
blood 22-1
Blythe, William Jefferson 31-41
bone fractures 23-4
book report 6-1
Boone, Daniel 33-3
Borglum, Gutzon 16-9
Boston Port Act 10-4
Boston Tea Party 10-3, 33-14
Boy Scouts of America 44-3
Boyce, William D. 44-3
Braille 34-2
Braille, Louis 34-2
brain 22-2
Brazil 13-3
Breckinridge, John C. 31-15
Brewster, David 45-4
bridges 41-3
Brown, John 10-9
Buchanan, James 31-15
Buddhism 35-1
Burkina Faso 13-4
Burr, Aaron 31-3
Burt, William Austin 41-23
Bush, Barbara 31-40
Bush, George Herbert Walker 31-39, **31-40**, 31-42
Bush, George Walker 31-42
Bush, Laura 31-42
butterfly 29-5
Byrd, Admiral Richard 32-2

C

Caballeros, Jerez de los 32-1
cactus 21-5
Caesar, Augustus 9-9, 45-6
Caesar, Julius 9-8
Caldecott Medal 1-8
calendars 8-5
Caley, George 45-5

Index | 147

Calhoun, John C. 31-6, 31-7
California 14-6
California Gold Rush 10-8
camel 25-3
cameras 41-4
Canada 13-5
capitalization 2-6
carnivorous plants 21-6
Carter, Howard 33-19
Carter, James Earl, Jr. 31-38
Carter, Rosalynn 31-38
Carver, George Washington 33-4
cat 25-4
caves 18-3
Cayley, George 40-1
cells 22-3
census 11-9
chameleon 27-4
Charbonneau 33-16
cheetah 25-5
Cheney, Richard B. 31-42
chess 44-5
chicken 26-7
children's book awards 1-8
Chile 13-6
chimpanzee 25-6
China 13-7
Chinese New Year 9-17
chocolate 38-1
Chopin, Frederic 43-3
Christianity 35-2
Christmas 9-40
cinquain poem 5-2
circus 44-6
Civil War, end of 10-17
Civil War uniforms 10-14
Clerc, Laurent 34-1
Cleveland, Frances 31-22
Cleveland, Grover 31-22
Cleveland, Ruth 31-22
clichés 4-6
Clinton, George 31-3
Clinton, Hillary 31-41
Clinton, William Jefferson 31-41
clocks 8-3
clouds 19-2
Cody, "Buffalo Bill" 33-5
Coleman, Ann 31-15
Colfax, Schuyler 31-18
colon 2-3
Colorado 14-7
colors 20-6
Columbus, Christopher 9-33, 26-7, 32-3, 32-9, 38-7
Columbus Day 9-33
comma 2-3
complex sentences 2-1

compound sentences 2-1
computer components 39-3
computer languages 39-5
computers, early 39-1
computers, types 39-2
condensation 20-9
Confucianism 35-3
Congreve, William 41-10
conjunctions 3-5
Connecticut 14-8
consonance 4-7
Constitution, U.S. 11-2, 11-3, 11-8
continents 12-1
Cook, James 14-12, 46-13
Coolidge, Calvin 16-9, 31-28, 31-29
Coolidge, Grace 31-29
Coretta Scott King Award 1-8
Cortés, Hernando 16-10, 32-4, 38-1
cotton gin 41-5
countries 13-1
Cousteau, Jacques 32-5
cow 25-7
Crazy Horse 10-21, 33-6
cricket 29-6
crocodile 27-3, 27-5
crossword puzzles 44-7
crustaceans 28-1
Curtis, Charles 31-30
Custer, George Armstrong 10-21, 33-6

D

D Day 9-27
Daguerre, Louis 41-4
Dallas, George 31-11
Dare, Virginia 14-34
dash 2-4
Davis, Jefferson 31-14
Dawes, Charles G. 31-29
days of the week 9-1
December 9-13
decimals 7-12
decimals, adding and subtracting 7-13
decimals, multiplying and dividing 7-14
Declaration of Independence 10-5
declarative sentence 2-2
Decoration Day 9-26
deer 25-8
Delaware 14-9
Democracy 11-1
Democratic Party 11-4
dentures 23-2
Dependency 11-1
deserts 15-3

Dewey Decimal Classification System (libraries) 1-10
Dewey Decimal Guide 1-11
Dewey, Melvil 1-10
diamanté poem 5-3
diaries 6-2
dice 44-8
dictionary 1-6
dinosaur, fossils 24-2
dinosaurs 24-1
dinosaurs, disappearance of 24-4
dinosaurs, types 24-3
dividing 7-6
division fun 7-8
Dodd, Mrs. John Bruce 9-29
dog 25-9
dogs in police work 25-10
dolphin 25-11
Douglas, Stephen A. 31-16
dowsing 36-10
dragonfly 29-7
dreams 36-11
Drebbel, Cornelius 40-8
Dreyfuss, Henry 41-18
drums 43-10

E

e-mail 39-8
eagle 26-6
ear 22-4
Earth 18-1
earthquakes 19-3
earthworm 30-2
echinoderms 30-3
echo 20-1
Edison, Thomas 33-7, 41-6
Edison's inventions 41-6
Edward I 7-20
Edward III 46-12
Egypt 13-8
Eiffel Tower 16-6
Eisenhower, Dwight D. 9-24, 31-33
Eisenhower, Mamie 31-33
Election Day 9-35
elephant 25-12
ellipsis 2-4
Ellis Island 10-22
Emancipation Proclamation 10-13
energy sources 20-2
equator 15-1
Europe 12-6
evaporation 20-9
exclamation point 2-4
exclamatory sentence 2-2
eye 22-5
eyeglasses 23-3

F

Fairbanks, Charles W. 31-25
Father's Day 9-29
Feather, William 1-5
feathers 26-3
feathers, types 26-4
February 9-3
Federal State 11-1
Ferdinand II 32-1
Festival of Lights 9-38
Fillmore, Abigail 31-13
Fillmore, Millard 31-12, **31-13**
fingerprints 22-6
firefly 29-8
fish 30-4
five senses 22-10
Flag Day 9-28
flag, U.S. 10-6
flamingo 26-8
flea 29-9
Florida 14-10
fly 29-10
folklore 36-2
foods, miscellaneous 38-8
football 46-4
Ford, Elizabeth ("Betty") 31-37
Ford, Gerald Rudolph 31-36, **31-37**
Ford, Henry 40-2
foreign terms 34-3, 34-4
fossils, dinosaur 24-2
Four Seasons by Vivaldi **43-4**
fractions 7-10
Franklin, Benjamin 8-3, 23-3, **33-8**, 44-12, 45-5
free verse 5-4
freezing 20-9
Fremont, John C. 11-5
Frisbee 45-2
frog 27-6, 27-7
Fu-tzu, K'ung 35-3

G

Gallaudet, Thomas Hopkins 34-1
Gandhi, Mahatma 38-5
Garfield, James Abram 31-20
Garfield, Lucretia 31-20
Garner, John N. 31-31
Gautama, Siddhartha 35-1
geometry 7-18
geometry formulas 7-19
Georgia 14-11
Gerry, Elbridge 31-4
Gettysburg Address 10-15
giraffe 25-13
Girl Scouts of America 44-3
glaciers 18-4

glass 41-7
Goldsmith, Oliver 1-5
golf 46-5
Gore, Albert A., Jr. 31-41
government, types 11-1
grammar exercises ("What's Wrong?") 2-9
Grant, Julia 31-18
Grant, Ulysses Simpson 10-17, 16-19, **31-18**
graphs 7-16
graphing fun 7-17
grasshopper 29-11
Great Chicago Fire 10-20
Great Depression 10-23
Greek goddesses 36-4
Greek gods 36-3
greeting cards 44-9
Grimm, Jacob and Wilhelm 36-2
Groundhog Day 9-18
Gruelle, Johnny 45-7
guinea pig 25-14
Guiteau, Charles 31-20
Gutenberg, Johannes 1-3
Gwin, William 10-10
Gwinnet, Button 44-4
gymnastics 46-6

H

haiku 5-5
Haines, Jackson 46-8
hair 22-7
Hale, Nathan 33-9
Halloween 9-34
Hamlin, Hannibal 31-16
Hanukkah 9-38
Harding, Florence 31-28
Harding, Warren Gamaliel 31-28
Harrison, Anna 31-9
Harrison, Benjamin 31-23
Harrison, Caroline 31-23
Harrison, William Henry 31-9
Hawaii 14-1, **14-12**
Hayes, Lucy 31-19
Hayes, Rutherford Berchard 31-19
heart 22-8
Heisman, John 46-4
Hendricks, Thomas A. 31-22
Henry I 7-20
Henry VIII 37-2
Henry, Edward Richard 22-6
hiccups 23-5
Hickock, "Wild Bill" 33-5
Hill, Patty and Mildred 43-1
Hillary, Edmund 32-6
Hinduism 35-4
hints for writers 6-5

hippopotamus 25-15
Hirohito, Emperor 35-7
Hobart, Garret A. 31-24
hockey 46-7
holograms 42-3
homonyms 4-2
Hoover, Herbert Clark 31-30
Hoover, Lou 31-30
Hopkinson, Francis 10-6
horse 25-16
hot air balloons 40-5
Houston, Sam 33-10
Hula Hoop 45-3
hummingbird 26-9
Humphrey, Hubert 31-35
Hunt, John 32-6
hurricanes 19-5
hyperbole 4-8
hyphen 2-4

I

ice cream 38-2
ice skating 46-8
icebergs 18-5
Idaho 14-13
idioms 4-9
igneous rock 18-8
Illinois 14-14
imperative sentence 2-2
Inauguration Day 9-16
Independence Day 9-30
Indiana 14-15
Indigenous Peoples Day 9-33
Indonesia 13-9
Industrial Revolution 10-2
insects 29-1
interjections 2-4, 3-6
Internet history 39-6
Internet address abbreviations 39-7
interrogative sentence 2-2
Intolerable Acts 10-4
invertebrates 30-5
Iowa 14-16
irregular verbs 3-13
Islam 35-5
islands 15-4

J

Jackson, Andrew 31-7
Jackson, Rachel 31-7
James I 40-8
January 9-2
Japan 13-10
Japanese relocation camps 10-25
Jarvis, Anna M. 9-25
Jefferson, Martha 31-3

Jefferson, Thomas 10-5, 11-4, 16-9, 31-2, **31-3**, 45-6
jellyfish 30-6
Jesus Christ 35-2
John Brown's Battle 10-9
Johnson, Andrew 31-16, **31-17**
Johnson, Claudia ("Lady Bird") 31-35
Johnson, Eliza 31-17
Johnson, Lyndon Baines 31-34, **31-35**
Johnson, Richard M. 31-8
jokes 44-10
journals 6-2
Judaism 35-6
July 9-8
jump ropes 44-11
June 9-7
Jupiter 17-1

K

kaleidoscope 45-4
kangaroo 25-17
Kansas 14-17
Kennedy, Jacqueline 31-34
Kennedy, John Fitzgerald 31-34, 31-41
Kentucky 14-18
key types 41-9
Key, Francis Scott 10-11
keyboard instruments 43-8
keys 41-8
Khan, Kublai 32-9
King Tut 33-19, 37-5
King, Billie Jean 33-15
King, Martin Luther, Jr. 9-15
King, William R. D. 31-14
kites 45-5
kiwi bird 26-10
koala 25-18
Kwanzaa 9-41

L

Labor Day 9-31
Lallement, Pierre 40-4
Lane, Harriet 31-15
Lao-tzu 35-9
lasers 20-4
laws, process of making 11-7
leaves 21-7
Lee, Robert E. 10-17, 31-18, **33-11**
left-handers 23-6
Lenoir, ftienne 40-2
Lewis and Clark expedition 33-16
Liberty Bell 16-7
libraries 1-9
library classification systems 1-10
Library of Congress 1-9

Library of Congress Classification System (libraries) 1-10
light 20-5
light year 7-21
lightning 19-6
lightning safety 19-7
limerick 5-6
Lincoln, Abraham 9-20, 10-13, 10-15, 16-9, **31-16**, 33-11, 33-18, 36-15, 44-13, 45-6
Lincoln, Mary Todd 31-16
lion 25-19
Lister, Thomas 16-7
Little Big Horn (battle) 10-21
lobster 28-4
Loch Ness Monster 36-12
loon 26-11
Louisiana 14-19
Lovelace, Augusta Ada 39-1
Low, Juliett 44-3

M

Madison, Dolley 31-4
Madison, James 31-4
Magellan, Ferdinand 32-7
magnetism 20-7
Maine 14-20
Mammoth Cave 18-3
Mann, Horace 33-12
manuscript books 1-2
maps 15-2
marbles 45-6
March 9-4
marionettes 42-8
Marley, Bob 43-2
Mars 17-2
Marshall, James 10-8
Marshall, Thomas R. 31-27
Martin Luther King, Jr.'s, Birthday 9-15
Maryland 14-21
Massachusetts 14-22
Massachusetts Government Act 10-4
matches 41-10
math facts 7-9
math mystery 7-11
May 9-6
May Day 9-23
McElory, Mary 31-21
McGuire, Peter J. 9-31
McKinley, Ida Saxton 31-24
McKinley, William 31-24
measurements 7-20
Medusa 36-13
melting 20-9
Memorial Day 9-26
Mercury (planet) 17-3

Merlin, Joseph 46-9
metamorphic rock 18-8
metaphors 4-10
metric measurements 7-22
Michelangelo 42-2, 42-9
Michigan 14-23
Michtom, Morris 45-11
million, how much is a 7-3
Minnesota 14-24
mirrors 41-11
Mississippi 14-25
Mississippi River 16-8
Missouri 14-26
Mohammed 35-5
mollusks 28-2
Monarchy 11-1
Mondale, Walter F. 31-38
money 41-12
Monroe, Elizabeth 31-5
Monroe, James 31-5
Montana 14-27
Montezuma 32-4, 38-1
Moon 17-10
moose 25-20
Morse code 34-5
Morse, Samuel 34-5
Morton, Levi P. 31-23
mosquito 29-12
moth 29-13
Mother's Day 9-25
motorcycles 40-6
Mount Rushmore 16-9
Mount St. Helens 19-13
mountains 15-4
Mozart 43-3
multiplying 7-6
multiplication fun 7-7
mummies, creating 10-1
music 43-1
music, African-American influenced 43-2
music, classical 43-3
music, folk 43-5
music, jazz 43-6
music, rock 43-7
myths 36-1

N

nails 41-13
Naismith, James 46-3
Nanak, Guru 35-8
National Archives 10-5
Nebraska 14-28
Neptune 17-4
nests, bird 26-2
Netherlands 13-11
Nevada 14-29
New Hampshire 14-30

New Jersey 14-31
New Mexico 14-32
New Year's Day 9-14
New York 14-33
New York City 11-8, 14-33, 16-13
Newbery Medal 1-8
Nixon, Patricia 31-36
Nixon, Richard Milhous 10-26, 31-33, **31-36**, 31-37
Normandy Coast (France) 9-27
North America 12-1, **12-7**
North Carolina 14-34
North Dakota 13-5, 14-1, **14-35**
northern lights (auroras) 19-8
nouns 3-7
November 9-12
nuclear energy 20-3
number magic 7-2
numbers 7-1

O

oceans 15-3, **18-6**
October 9-11
octopus 28-5
Ohio 14-36
Oklahoma 14-37
onomatopoeia 4-11
Oregon 14-38
ostrich 26-12
Owen, Richard 24-1
oyster 28-6

P

painters 42-2
paintings, types 42-1
Panama Canal 16-10
pantomime 42-7
paper 41-14
parentheses 2-5
parts of speech 3-1
Paterson, Katherine 1-5
pattern poetry 5-7
Pavlov, Ivan 33-13
Pearl Harbor, attack on 10-24
Pearl Harbor Day 9-39
pearls 28-6
pencils 41-15
penguin 26-13
Pennsylvania 14-39
percussion instruments 43-9
period 2-5
personification 4-12
Philadelphia, Pennsylvania 11-2, 11-5, 11-8
Philips, Alonzo D. 41-10
Phoenicians 1-1
phrenology 36-14
Picasso, Pablo 42-2

Pierce, Franklin 31-14
Pierce, Jane 31-14
Pizarro, Francisco 32-8
plants, parts of 21-1
Plato 23-6, 36-7
platypus 25-21
play, elements of 42-6
playing cards 44-12
Pluto 17-5
Plymouth Rock 16-11
poetry 5-1
polar bear 25-22
Polk, James Knox 10-8, 16-13, **31-11**
Polk, Sara 31-11
Polo, Marco 32-9
Ponce de Leõn, Juan 32-10
Pony Express 10-10
popcorn 38-3
porcupine 25-23
postcards 44-13
Prang, Louis 44-9
premonitions 36-15
prepositions 3-9
President, qualifications 11-6
Presidents' Day 9-20
Presley, Elvis 44-4
pretzels 38-4
printing 1-3
Promontory Point, Utah 10-19
pronouns 3-10
proper nouns 3-8
Ptolemy I 1-9
Punch and Judy 42-8
punctuation 2-3, 2-4, 2-5
puppets and marionettes 42-8
Putnam, Herbert 1-10
pyramids 16-12

Q

Quayle, J. Danforth 31-40
question mark 2-5
quinzaine poem 5-8
quotation marks 2-5
quotations 1-5

R

Raggedy Ann 45-7
rain 19-9
rain forests 18-7
rainbows 19-10
Reagan, Nancy 31-39
Reagan, Ronald Wilson 31-39

relocation camps 10-25
reminiscences 6-2
reports 6-3
reptiles 27-2
Republic 11-1
Republican Party 11-5
respiratory system 22-9
Revere, Paul 33-14
Rheims, France 9-24
Rhode Island 14-1, **14-40**, 18-3
Ricketts, Bill 44-6
riddles 44-14
Ride, Sally 33-15
rivers 15-3
roach 29-14
robots 41-16
Rockefeller, Nelson A. 31-37
rockets 41-17
rocks 18-8
Rockwell, Norman 42-2
roller skates 46-9
Roman goddesses 9-6, 9-7, **36-6**
Roman gods 9-1, 9-2, 9-4, **36-5**
Roman numerals 7-4
Roosevelt, (Anna) Eleanor 31-31
Roosevelt, Edith 31-25
Roosevelt, Franklin Delano 9-39, 10-25, 11-6, **31-31**, 41-12
Roosevelt, Theodore 16-9, 31-24, **31-25**, 31-27, 45-11, 46-4
Rosh Hashanah 9-32
Ross, Betsy 10-6
Ross, Nellie Tayloe 14-51

S

Sacajawea 33-16
salt 38-5
Sampson, Deborah 33-17
San Francisco Earthquake 19-4
sandwiches 38-6
Saturn 17-6
savings and "piggy" banks 45-8
Schubert, Franz 43-3
scuba diving 46-10
sculpture 42-4
sea horse 30-7
sedimentary rock 18-8
seeds 21-2
seeds, spreading 21-3
semaphore 34-6
semicolon 2-5
sentences 2-1, 2-2
September 9-10
Seven Wonders of the Ancient World 16-1
Seven Wonders of the World 16-2
Seward, William H. 10-18
"Seward's Folly" 10-18

shark 30-8
shells 28-7
Sherman's March to Atlanta 10-16
Sherman, James S. 31-26
Sherman, William Tecumseh 10-16
Shinto 35-7
Shippen, Peggy 33-2
"Shurtlieff, Robert" 33-17
shoes 37-2
Siedwi 46-8
Sikhism 35-8
Silly Putty 45-9
similes 4-13
simple sentences 2-1
skiing, snow 46-11
skin 22-11
skunk 25-24
Slinky 45-10
Smithsonian Institution 16-13
snail 28-8
snake 27-8
snoring 23-7
soap bubbles 20-10
soccer 46-12
software 39-4
Soto, Hernando de 32-11
South Africa 13-12
South America 12-1, **12-8**
South Carolina 14-41
South Dakota 14-1, **14-42**, 16-9
space travel 40-7
speeches 6-4
spelling rules 2-7, 2-8
spices 38-7
St. Patrick's Day 9-21
St. Valentine's Day 9-19
stamps 44-15
"Star Spangled Banner" 10-11
starfish 30-9
stars 17-11
states 14-1
states of matter 20-8
states of matter, changing 20-9
Statue of Liberty 16-14
statues 42-9
Stevenson, Adlai 31-22
Stonehenge 16-15
Stradivarius, Antonio 43-11
stringed instruments 43-11
submarines 40-8
subtracting 7-5
Sun 17-9
sundial 8-2
superstitions 36-16
Supreme Court 11-8
surfing 46-13
Sutter, John 10-8
synonyms 4-3

T

Taft, Helen 31-26
Taft, William Howard 31-26
Taoism 35-9
tattoos 37-3
Taylor, Margaret 31-12
Taylor, Zachary 31-12
teddy bear 45-11
teeth 22-12
telephone 41-18
telescopes 41-19
television 41-20
Tennessee 14-43
tennis 46-14
Tensing, Sherpa 32-6
termite 29-15
Texas 14-44
Thailand 13-13
Thanksgiving 9-37
thermometer 41-21
thesaurus 1-7
Tilden, Samuel J. 31-19
time, intervals 8-1
toad 27-7
Tompkins, Daniel D. 31-5
tongue 22-13
tongue twisters 4-14
tornadoes 19-11
traffic signals 41-22
trains 40-9
Transcontinental Railroad 10-19
Trevithick, Richard 40-9
Truman, Elizabeth 31-32
Truman, Harry S. 9-16, 31-31, 31-32
Truth, Sojourner 33-18
Tubman, Harriet 10-12
turkey, wild 26-14
Tutankhamen 33-19
Twain, Mark 16-8, 41-23
twins 23-8
Tyler, John 31-9, **31-10**
Tyler, Julia 31-10
Tyler, Letitia 31-10
typewriter 41-23

U

umbrellas 37-4
Underground Railroad 10-12
underwear 37-5
unicorns 36-17
unidentified flying objects (UFOs) 36-18
Uranus 17-7
Utah 14-45

V

V-E Day 9-24
Valley Forge 10-7
Van Buren, Hannah 31-8
Van Buren, Martin 31-7, **31-8**
Vatican City 13-14
Venus 17-8
verb tenses 3-12
verbs 3-11
Vermont 14-46
Veteran's Day 9-36
Vietnam Veterans Memorial 16-16
Vinci, Leonardo da 23-3, 42-2, 42-9
Virgina 14-47
Vivaldi, Antonio 43-4
volcanoes 19-12

W

Walker, John 41-10
Wallace, Henry A. 31-31
Washington (state) 14-48
Washington, DC 1-9, 9-15, 10-5, 10-26, 11-8, 14-1, 16-13, 16-16
Washington Monument 16-17
Washington, George 9-16, 9-20, 10-7, 11-2, 16-7, 16-18, 23-2, **31-1**, 31-5, 40-5, 45-6
Washington, Martha 31-1
watches 8-4
Watergate 10-26
weather vanes 19-14
Webster, Noah 1-6
Welles, Orson 36-18
Wells, H. G. 36-18
West Virginia 14-49
whale 25-25
"What's Wrong?" (grammar exercises) 2-9
Wheeler, William A. 31-19
White, E. B. 1-5
White House 16-18
Whitney, Eli 41-5
Williams, Roger 14-40
Wilson, Edith 31-27
Wilson, Ellen 31-27
Wilson, Henry 31-18
Wilson, Woodrow 31-27
wind instruments 43-12
Wisconsin 14-50
wolf 25-26
Wright, Wilbur 40-1
Wright, Orville 40-1
Wyoming 14-51

Y

Yellowstone National Park 16-19
yo-yo 45-12
Yom Kippur 9-32

Z

Zoroastrianism 35-10

www.ingramcontent.com/pod-product-compliance
Lightning Source LLC
Chambersburg PA
CBHW080540300426
44111CB00017B/2818